Company's Coming ®

ONE-DISH MEALS

by
Jean Paré

www.**company's**coming.com
visit our web-site

Dedication

One-dish meals . . .
All for one, and one for all!

Cover Photo

1. Chicken Vinaigrette, page 105

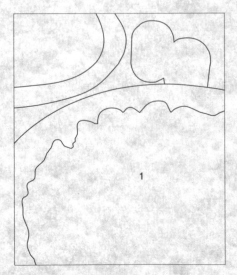

Props Courtesy Of: C C on Whyte, Dansk Gifts,
Handworks Gallery,
La Cache, The Bay

ONE-DISH MEALS

Eighth Printing May 2002

Canadian Cataloguing in Publication Data

Paré, Jean
One-Dish Meals

Issued also in French under title: Des repas en un plat
Includes index.
ISBN 1-895455-54-5

1. Entrées (Cookery). I. Title.

TX693.P376 1999   641.8'12   C99-900195-7

Published and Distributed by
Company's Coming Publishing Limited
2311 - 96 Street
Edmonton, Alberta, Canada T6N 1G3
www.companyscoming.com

**Published Simultaneously in
Canada and the United States of America**

Printed In Canada

Company's Coming Cookbooks

Original Series

- 150 Delicious Squares
- Casseroles
- Muffins & More
- Salads
- Appetizers
- Desserts
- Soups & Sandwiches
- Cookies
- Main Courses
- Pasta
- Barbecues
- Light Recipes
- Preserves
- Light Casseroles
- Chicken
- Kids Cooking
- Breads
- Meatless Cooking
- Cooking For Two
- Breakfasts & Brunches
- Slow Cooker Recipes
- One Dish Meals
- Starters
- Stir-Fry
- Make-Ahead Meals
- The Potato Book
- Low-Fat Cooking
- Low-Fat Pasta
- Appliance Cooking
- Cook For Kids
- Stews, Chilies & Chowders
- Fondues
- The Beef Book
- Asian Cooking
- The Cheese Book
- The Rookie Cook **NEW** July 1/02

Greatest Hits Series

- Biscuits, Muffins & Loaves
- Dips, Spreads & Dressings
- Soups & Salads
- Sandwiches & Wraps
- Italian
- Mexican

Lifestyle Series

- Grilling
- Diabetic Cooking

Special Occasion Series

- Chocolate Everything
- Gifts from the Kitchen
- Cooking for the Seasons

table of Contents

The Jean Paré Story 6

Foreword 7

Beef 8

Eggs 40

Fish & Seafood... 46

Meatless 61

Pork & Lamb.. 66

Poultry 92

Salads 120

Soups 137

Measurement Tables 151

Index... 152

Mail Order Form 159

the Jean Paré story

Jean Paré grew up understanding that the combination of family, friends and home cooking is the essence of a good life. From her mother she learned to appreciate good cooking, while her father praised even her earliest attempts. When she left home she took with her many acquired family recipes, her love of cooking and her intriguing desire to read recipe books like novels!

In 1963, when her four children had all reached school age, Jean volunteered to cater to the 50th anniversary of the Vermilion School of Agriculture, now Lakeland College. Working out of her home, Jean prepared a dinner for over 1000 people which launched a flourishing catering operation that continued for over eighteen years. During that time she was provided with countless opportunities to test new ideas with immediate feedback—resulting in empty plates and contented customers! Whether preparing cocktail sandwiches for a house party or serving a hot meal for 1500 people, Jean Paré earned a reputation for good food, courteous service and reasonable prices.

"Why don't you write a cookbook?" Time and again, as requests for her recipes mounted, Jean was asked that question. Jean's response was to team up with her son, Grant Lovig, in the fall of 1980 to form Company's Coming Publishing Limited. April 14, 1981, marked the debut of "150 DELICIOUS SQUARES", the first Company's Coming cookbook in what soon would become Canada's most popular cookbook series.

Jean Paré's operation has grown steadily from the early days of working out of a spare bedroom in her home. Full-time staff includes marketing personnel located in major cities across Canada. Home Office is based in Edmonton, Alberta in a modern building constructed specially for the company.

Today the company distributes throughout Canada and the United States in addition to numerous overseas markets, all under the guidance of Jean's daughter, Gail Lovig. Best-sellers many times over in English, Company's Coming cookbooks have also been published in French and Spanish. Familiar and trusted in home kitchens the world over, Company's Coming cookbooks are offered in a variety of formats, including the original softcover series.

Jean Paré's approach to cooking has always called for quick and easy recipes using everyday ingredients. Even when travelling, she is constantly on the lookout for new ideas to share with her readers. At home, she can usually be found researching and writing recipes, or working in the company's test kitchen. Jean continues to gain new supporters by adhering to what she calls "the golden rule of cooking": never share a recipe you wouldn't use yourself. It's an approach that works—*millions of times over!*

Foreword

One-Dish Meals features a variety of recipes that can be prepared in a casserole dish, roaster, Dutch oven, slow cooker, large saucepan, electric or other frying pan, or even a large salad bowl. Oven cooking as well as stove top cooking offers you more choice in how you would like to prepare your dish. Some recipes are prepared completely in one container, while others require more than one to prepare but are served in one dish.

Cooking in one dish saves time, uses less fuel, and cleanup is a breeze. Even with recipes that are prepared in several steps, cleanup can be done as you go. Here is the perfect opportunity to double your favorite recipe and put half into the freezer.

To complete these meals, try adding a salad, dinner rolls and dessert. If a recipe is very hearty, you may choose to skip either the salad or the rolls. On the other hand, if extra people turn up at mealtime you can stretch any recipe by serving not only a salad but also an extra vegetable to complement your main dish. The addition of garlic toast or baking powder biscuits goes particularly well with a lighter one-dish meal.

Want to keep it simple? One-Dish Meals is a helpful collection of easy-to-serve mealtime ideas—perfect for when company's coming!

Jean Paré

Each recipe has been analyzed using the most up-to-date version of the Canadian Nutrient File from Health Canada, which is based on the United States Department of Agriculture (USDA) Nutrient Data Base. If more that one ingredient is listed (such as "hard margarine or butter"), then the first ingredient is used in the analysis. Where an ingredient reads "sprinkle", "optional", or "for garnish", it is not included as part of the nutrition information.

Margaret Ng, B.Sc. (Hon), M.A.
Registered Dietitian

SAUCY SKILLET DINNER

This is a very easy all-in-one dish. Rich tasting and thick.

Lean ground beef	1 lb.	454 g
Chopped onion	1 cup	250 mL
Garlic clove, minced (or ¼ tsp., 1 mL, powder)	1	1
Medium zucchini, with peel, halved lengthwise and sliced	1	1
Chopped fresh mushrooms	1 cup	250 mL
Water	1 cup	250 mL
Spaghetti sauce	2 cups	500 mL
Dried sweet basil	½ tsp.	2 mL
Granulated sugar	½ tsp.	2 mL
Dried whole oregano, just a pinch		
Uncooked spaghetti, broken into 1-2 inch (2.5-5 cm) lengths	6 oz.	170 g
Grated part-skim mozzarella cheese	½ cup	125 mL

Scramble-fry ground beef, onion and garlic in large non-stick frying pan for 3 to 4 minutes.

Add zucchini and mushrooms. Cook for 6 to 7 minutes, stirring occasionally, until beef is no longer pink. Drain.

Add water, spaghetti sauce, basil, sugar and oregano. Heat until boiling. Add pasta. Reduce heat. Cover. Simmer for 20 minutes until pasta is tender but firm and liquid is mostly absorbed.

Add mozzarella cheese. Stir until melted. Serves 4.

1 serving: 451 Calories; 13.7 g Total Fat; 825 mg Sodium; 32 g Protein; 50 g Carbohydrate; 5 g Dietary Fiber

Paré Pointer

There is no question as to what dinosaurs eat. They eat anything they want.

This has the popular taco seasoning with a touch of chili powder which may easily be increased. Very tasty.

Lean ground beef	1 lb.	454 g
Finely chopped onion	1 cup	250 mL
Chopped green pepper	1 cup	250 mL
Garlic salt	1 tsp.	5 mL
Pepper	$\frac{1}{8}$ tsp.	0.5 mL
Canned stewed tomatoes, with juice, broken up	2 × 14 oz.	2 × 398 mL
Canned kernel corn, with liquid	12 oz.	341 mL
Envelope taco seasoning mix	1 × 1¼ oz.	1 × 35 g
Granulated sugar	1 tsp.	5 mL
Chili powder (or more to taste)	$\frac{1}{2}$ tsp.	2 mL
Water	$\frac{1}{2}$ cup	125 mL
Uncooked long grain white rice	$\frac{2}{3}$ cup	150 mL
Grated medium Cheddar cheese	$\frac{1}{2}$ cup	125 mL
Light sour cream	$\frac{3}{4}$ cup	175 mL
Sliced pitted ripe olives	$\frac{1}{4}$ cup	60 mL
Corn chips, for garnish (optional)	1 cup	250 mL

Scramble-fry first 5 ingredients in large non-stick frying pan until onion is soft and beef is no longer pink. Drain.

Stir in next 7 ingredients. Cover. Simmer for about 20 minutes, stirring occasionally, until rice is tender and liquid is absorbed. Turn into serving dish.

Sprinkle with cheese. Dab sour cream over top. Sprinkle with olives. Add corn chips here and there. Serves 4.

1 serving: 566 Calories; 19.6 g Total Fat; 2289 mg Sodium; 33 g Protein; 69 g Carbohydrate; 6 g Dietary Fiber

Pictured on page 17.

Paré Pointer

There weren't nearly so many accidents when horsepower was with the horses.

MEAT AND POTATOES

A slow cooker is required for this ground beef stew.

Medium potatoes, thinly sliced	4	4
Sliced carrot	2 cups	500 mL
Chopped onion	2 cups	500 mL
Frozen peas (about 10 oz., 285 g)	2 cups	500 mL
Salt, sprinkle		
Pepper, sprinkle		
Condensed cream of chicken soup	10 oz.	284 mL
Water	1 cup	250 mL
Liquid gravy browner	¼-½ tsp.	1-2 mL
Lean ground beef	1½ lbs.	680 g

Layer first 4 ingredients in order given in 5 quart (5 L) slow cooker, sprinkling each layer with salt and pepper.

Mix soup, water and gravy browner in medium bowl.

Add ground beef. Mix well. Place over vegetables. Cover. Cook on Low for 10 to 12 hours or on High for 5 to 6 hours. Makes 13 cups (3.25 L).

1½ cups (375 mL): 296 Calories; 14.2 g Total Fat; 383 mg Sodium; 19 g Protein; 23 g Carbohydrate; 4 g Dietary Fiber

COMFORT CHILI

This is more beany than meaty. Even better flavor when reheated the next day. Very nutritious.

Lean ground beef	1 lb.	454 g
Chopped onion	1 cup	250 mL
Chopped celery	1 cup	250 mL
Small green pepper, chopped	1	1
Canned diced tomatoes, drained	14 oz.	398 mL
Canned kidney beans, drained	3 × 14 oz.	3 × 398 mL
Condensed cream of mushroom soup	10 oz.	284 mL
Chili powder	1 tbsp.	15 mL
Garlic salt	1 tsp.	5 mL
Pepper	½ tsp.	2 mL

(continued on next page)

Scramble-fry ground beef, onion, celery and green pepper in large pot or Dutch oven until beef is no longer pink. Drain.

Add remaining 6 ingredients. Bring to a boil. Reduce heat. Simmer, uncovered, for 1 hour, stirring often to prevent burning. Makes 8 cups (2 L).

1½ cups (375 mL): 388 Calories; 12.5 g Total Fat; 1205 mg Sodium; 29 g Protein; 42 g Carbohydrate; 12 g Dietary Fiber

EASY TACO SUPPER

Fast, easy and so good.

Lean ground beef	1 lb.	454 g
Chopped onion	½ cup	125 mL
Chopped green pepper	½ cup	125 mL
Hot water	2½ cups	625 mL
Envelope taco seasoning mix	1 × 1¼ oz.	1 × 35 g
Package macaroni and cheese dinner, cheese-flavored packet reserved	6½ oz.	200 g
Reserved cheese-flavored packet Diced tomato	1 cup	250 mL
Non-fat sour cream (optional)	½ cup	125 mL
Thinly sliced green onion (optional)	¼ cup	60 mL
Shredded lettuce (optional)	2 cups	500 mL

Scramble-fry ground beef, onion and green pepper in large non-stick frying pan for about 5 minutes until onion is soft and beef is no longer pink. Drain.

Stir in hot water and taco seasoning mix. Bring to a boil. Stir in macaroni from package. Cover. Simmer, stirring occasionally, for 7 to 8 minutes until macaroni is tender.

Add reserved cheese-flavored packet and tomato. Stir together well.

Serve immediately with sour cream, green onion and lettuce. Serves 6.

1 serving: 275 Calories; 8.1 g Total Fat; 691 mg Sodium; 20 g Protein; 31 g Carbohydrate; 1 g Dietary Fiber

MACARONI HASH

An interesting mix. Rich looking and full of beans. Goes well with the macaroni. Very flavorful.

Lean ground beef	1 lb.	454 g
Chopped onion	1 cup	250 mL
Chopped green pepper	¼ cup	60 mL
Elbow macaroni	1½ cups	375 mL
Boiling water	2½ qts.	2.5 L
Cooking oil (optional)	2 tsp.	10 mL
Salt	1 tsp.	5 mL
Tomato sauce	2 × 7½ oz.	2 × 213 mL
Chili powder (or more to taste)	1½ tsp.	7 mL
Salt	1 tsp.	5 mL
Canned kidney beans, drained	14 oz.	398 mL
Frozen kernel corn	1 cup	250 mL
Grated medium Cheddar cheese	1 cup	250 mL

Combine ground beef, onion and green pepper in large non-stick frying pan. Sauté until onion is soft and beef is no longer pink. Drain.

Cook pasta in boiling water, cooking oil and salt in large uncovered pot or Dutch oven for 5 to 7 minutes, stirring occasionally, until tender but firm. Drain. Return pasta to pot.

Add tomato sauce, chili powder and salt to beef mixture. Cook, uncovered, for 10 to 12 minutes until thickened.

Add kidney beans. Stir together. Turn into ungreased 2 quart (2 L) casserole.

Sprinkle with corn. Spread macaroni over corn.

Sprinkle cheese over macaroni. Cover. Bake in 350°F (175°C) oven for 25 minutes. Remove cover. Bake for 5 minutes until cheese is melted. Serves 6.

1 serving: 407 Calories; 14 g Total Fat; 1149 mg Sodium; 28 g Protein; 44 g Carbohydrate; 6 g Dietary Fiber

Pictured on page 53.

A homemade TV dinner.

BEEF PATTIES

Non-fat sour cream	⅔ cup	150 mL
Finely chopped onion	⅓ cup	75 mL
Coarsely crushed corn flakes cereal	⅔ cup	150 mL
Pepper	¼ tsp.	1 mL
Beef bouillon powder	1 tsp.	5 mL
Lean ground beef	1 lb.	454 g
Cooking oil	1 tsp.	5 mL
Frozen green beans	2¼ cups	560 mL
Elbow macaroni	1½ cups	375 mL
Boiling water	2 qts.	2 L
Salt	1 tsp.	5 mL
Condensed tomato soup	10 oz.	284 mL
Beef bouillon powder	1 tbsp.	15 mL
Water	½ cup	125 mL
Pepper	¼ tsp.	1 mL
Onion powder	¼ tsp.	1 mL

Beef Patties: Mix first 5 ingredients in medium bowl. Add ground beef. Mix. Let stand for 15 minutes. Shape into 8 patties. Remove patties and blot on paper towel.

Heat cooking oil in large frying pan. Add patties. Cook both sides until browned and no longer pink inside.

Cook green beans and pasta in boiling water and salt in large uncovered saucepan for 5 to 7 minutes, stirring occasionally, until pasta is tender but firm. Drain. Turn into ungreased 9 x 13 inch (22 x 33 cm) pan or casserole large enough to hold beef patties in single layer. Arrange patties over top.

Mix remaining 5 ingredients in small bowl. Pour over top. Cover. Bake in 350°F (175°C) oven for 20 to 30 minutes until bubbly hot. Serves 4.

1 serving: 500 Calories; 12.9 g Total Fat; 1347 mg Sodium; 31 g Protein; 65 g Carbohydrate; 3 g Dietary Fiber

Pictured on page 53.

ORIENTAL BEEF DINNER

This lends itself to variations. Sliced water chestnuts or bamboo shoots can be added.

Lean ground beef	½ lb.	225 g
Chopped onion	½ cup	125 mL
Sliced celery	½ cup	125 mL
Uncooked long grain white rice	½ cup	125 mL
Canned sliced mushrooms, with liquid	10 oz.	284 mL
Soy sauce	2 tbsp.	30 mL
Beef bouillon powder	1 tsp.	5 mL
Garlic powder	⅛ tsp.	0.5 mL
Pepper, sprinkle		
Hot water	1 cup	250 mL
Frozen pea pods	6 oz.	170 g
Fresh bean sprouts (about 2 large handfuls), coarsely chopped	2 cups	500 mL
Cornstarch	1 tsp.	5 mL
Water	1 tbsp.	15 mL
Chili sauce	1 tbsp.	15 mL

Scramble-fry ground beef and onion in large non-stick frying pan until onion is soft and beef is no longer pink. Drain.

Add next 8 ingredients. Stir together. Cover. Simmer for 15 minutes.

Add pea pods and bean sprouts. Stir together.

Mix cornstarch and water in small cup. Add chili sauce. Stir into beef mixture until boiling. Makes 6 cups (1.5 L).

1½ cups (375 mL): 244 Calories; 5.3 g Total Fat; 920 mg Sodium; 17 g Protein; 33 g Carbohydrate; 4 g Dietary Fiber

Paré Pointer

Golfers never starve; they live on the greens.

An all-in-one meal. Spices add pizzazz to the taste.

Lean ground beef	1 lb.	454 g
Chopped onion	½ cup	125 mL
Chopped celery	½ cup	125 mL
Seasoning salt	1¼ tsp.	6 mL
Pepper, sprinkle		
All-purpose flour	1 tbsp.	15 mL
Uncooked elbow macaroni	1¾ cups	425 mL
Thinly sliced zucchini, with peel	2 cups	500 mL
Canned stewed tomatoes, with juice, blended	28 oz.	796 mL
Dried whole oregano	1 tsp.	5 mL
Granulated sugar	½ tsp.	2 mL
Hot pepper sauce	½ tsp.	2 mL
Salt	¼ tsp.	1 mL
Pepper, sprinkle		
Bread slices, processed into crumbs (about 1½ cups, 375 mL)	2	2
Grated light medium Cheddar cheese	½ cup	125 mL

Scramble-fry ground beef, onion and celery in medium non-stick frying pan until onion is soft and beef is no longer pink. Drain.

Sprinkle with seasoning salt, pepper and flour. Mix well. Place beef mixture in bottom of lightly greased 3 quart (3 L) casserole.

Cover with pasta. Layer zucchini over pasta.

Combine tomatoes with juice, oregano, sugar, hot pepper sauce, salt and pepper in small bowl. Pour over zucchini.

Combine bread crumbs and cheese in small bowl. Sprinkle over surface of casserole. Bake, uncovered, in 350°F (175°C) oven for 50 to 55 minutes until pasta is tender and casserole is bubbling and browned. Cover with piece of foil if bread crumbs become too brown before pasta is cooked. Let stand for 10 minutes to absorb any excess liquid. Serves 6.

1 serving: 348 Calories; 9.4 g Total Fat; 914 mg Sodium; 23 g Protein; 43 g Carbohydrate; 4 g Dietary Fiber

LAZY CABBAGE ROLL CASSEROLE

Get the flavor without all the work.

Bacon slices, diced	4	4
Lean ground beef	1½ lbs.	680 g
Chopped onion	1 cup	250 mL
Condensed tomato soup	10 oz.	284 mL
Canned tomato juice	10 oz.	284 mL
Salt	½ tsp.	2 mL
Pepper	¼ tsp.	1 mL
Coarsely shredded cabbage	8 cups	2 L
Uncooked long grain white rice	⅓ cup	75 mL

Cook bacon in large frying pan until browned. Drain. Remove to plate.

Scramble-fry ground beef and onion in same frying pan until onion is soft and beef is no longer pink. Drain.

Add soup, tomato juice, salt and pepper. Stir.

Layer cabbage in ungreased 9 x 13 inch (22 x 33 cm) pan. Pack down. Sprinkle with rice. Scatter bacon over rice. Spoon beef mixture over top. Cover. Bake in 350°F (175°C) oven for about 1½ hours. Serves 6.

1 serving: *312 Calories; 12.6 g Total Fat; 876 mg Sodium; 25 g Protein; 25 g Carbohydrate; 3 g Dietary Fiber*

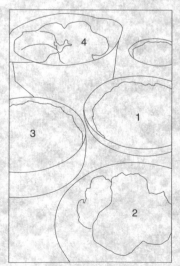

1. Tamale Rice Dish, page 9
2. Tuna Frills, page 46
3. Spicy Sausage And Pasta, page 79
4. Stove Top Pot Pie, page 26

Props Courtesy Of: Dansk Gifts, Eaton's,
Handworks Gallery,
The Bay, X/S Wares

CAPPELLETTI CASSEROLE

Additional helpers added to the ground beef. Good dish. This pasta looks like little hats.

Lean ground beef	1½ lbs.	680 g
Chopped onion	1½ cups	375 mL
Chopped celery	½ cup	125 mL
Cooking oil	1 tsp.	5 mL
Uncooked cappelletti pasta (8 oz., 225 g)	2⅔ cups	650 mL
Frozen peas (about 10 oz., 285 g)	2 cups	500 mL
Beef bouillon powder	2 tsp.	10 mL
Worcestershire sauce	1 tsp.	5 mL
Condensed cream of mushroom soup	10 oz.	284 mL
Condensed tomato soup	10 oz.	284 mL
Water	½ cup	125 mL
Grated medium Cheddar cheese	1 cup	250 mL

Scramble-fry ground beef, onion and celery in cooking oil in large non-stick frying pan until onion is soft and beef is no longer pink. Drain. Turn into ungreased 3 quart (3 L) casserole.

Add next 4 ingredients. Stir together.

Mix both soups and water in small bowl. Add to pasta mixture. Mix well, making sure pasta is covered.

Sprinkle with cheese. Cover. Bake in 350°F (175°C) oven for about 1½ hours. Makes 8 cups (2 L).

1½ cups (375 mL): 579 Calories; 26.6 g Total Fat; 1521 mg Sodium; 40 g Protein; 45 g Carbohydrate; 4 g Dietary Fiber

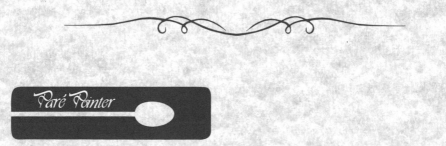

Paré Pointer

Sign on an optician's window: If you don't see what you want, you need my help.

MEATLOAF CASSEROLE

Mellow and flavorful as well as a very different presentation.

Large egg, fork-beaten	1	1
Milk	½ cup	125 mL
Rolled oats (not instant)	½ cup	125 mL
Finely chopped onion	1 cup	250 mL
Grated Parmesan cheese	2 tbsp.	30 mL
Beef bouillon powder	2 tsp.	10 mL
Worcestershire sauce	1 tsp.	5 mL
Salt	½ tsp.	2 mL
Pepper	¼ tsp.	1 mL
Lean ground beef	1½ lbs.	680 g
Ketchup	2 tbsp.	30 mL
Medium carrots, cut bite size	6	6
Medium potatoes	6	6
Water, to cover		
Hot milk	½ cup	125 mL
Salt, sprinkle		
Pepper, sprinkle		
Frozen peas	2 cups	500 mL
Water, to cover		
Grated medium Cheddar cheese	½ cup	125 mL

Combine first 9 ingredients in medium bowl. Stir together.

Mix in ground beef. Shape into loaf. Place in center of ungreased 9 x 13 inch (22 x 33 cm) pan.

Spread ketchup over top of loaf.

Arrange carrot around loaf. Bake, uncovered, in 350°F (175°C) oven for 1½ hours. Drain off any liquid.

Cook potatoes in water until tender. Drain.

Mash potatoes, adding hot milk, salt and pepper.

Cook peas in water for about 3 minutes. Drain. Spoon over carrot. Spoon mashed potato over vegetables around meatloaf.

(continued on next page)

Sprinkle potato with cheese. Return to oven for about 10 minutes until cheese is melted. Serves 6.

1 serving: 464 Calories; 15.5 g Total Fat; 779 mg Sodium; 34 g Protein; 48 g Carbohydrate; 7 g Dietary Fiber

MEXICAN CORN CHIP CASSEROLE

Use less jalapeño pepper or omit altogether if you need to keep the "heat" down.

Lean ground beef	1 lb.	454 g
Garlic clove, minced	1	1
Chopped onion	½ cup	125 mL
Chopped green pepper	½ cup	125 mL
Chopped fresh parsley	½ cup	125 mL
Medium tomatoes, diced	3	3
Tomato sauce	7½ oz.	213 mL
Fresh (or canned) jalapeño pepper, finely diced (wear rubber gloves)	1	1
Ground cumin	1 tsp.	5 mL
Chili powder	¼ tsp.	1 mL
Canned pinto beans, drained	14 oz.	398 mL
Broken corn chips	2 cups	500 mL
Grated Monterey Jack cheese	½ cup	125 mL
Grated medium Cheddar cheese	½ cup	125 mL

Scramble-fry ground beef, garlic, onion, green pepper and parsley in large non-stick frying pan for about 5 minutes until beef is no longer pink. Drain.

Add tomato, tomato sauce and jalapeño pepper. Sauté until jalapeño pepper is soft and mixture is simmering.

Add cumin and chili powder. Stir together well. Simmer for 10 minutes. Remove from heat.

Add pinto beans. Stir. Pour into lightly greased 2 quart (2 L) casserole.

Sprinkle corn chips and both cheeses over top. Bake, uncovered, in 350°F (175°C) oven for 30 minutes. Serves 6.

1 serving: 387 Calories; 19.5 g Total Fat; 618 mg Sodium; 24 g Protein; 30 g Carbohydrate; 4 g Dietary Fiber

AUTUMN BAKE

Very attractive and appetizing.

Medium potatoes, quartered lengthwise	4-5	4-5
Water, to cover		
Salt	¾ tsp.	4 mL
Pepper	¼ tsp.	1 mL
All-purpose flour	¼ cup	60 mL
Beef sirloin steak, cut into paper-thin strips	1¼ lbs.	568 g
Cooking oil	2 tsp.	10 mL
Salt, sprinkle		
Pepper, sprinkle		
Small zucchini, with peel, sliced to cover	1	1
Large tomatoes, sliced to cover	2	2
Dried whole oregano	½ tsp.	2 mL
Dried sweet basil	½ tsp.	2 mL
Onion powder	½ tsp.	2 mL
Hard margarine (or butter)	4 tsp.	20 mL
Dry bread crumbs	½ cup	125 mL
Grated part-skim mozzarella cheese	1 cup	250 mL

Cook potato in water in medium saucepan for 5 minutes. Drain. When cool enough to handle, slice.

Mix salt and pepper and flour in medium bowl. Add sliced potato. Toss together to coat. Place potato in greased 3 quart (3 L) casserole.

Brown steak strips in cooking oil in medium frying pan. Sprinkle with salt and pepper. Layer over potato.

Add layers of zucchini and tomato.

Mix oregano, basil and onion powder in small cup. Sprinkle over top.

Melt margarine in small saucepan. Stir in bread crumbs and cheese. Sprinkle over all. Cover. Bake in 350°F (175°C) oven for about 1 hour. Serves 4.

1 serving: 511 Calories; 17.7 g Total Fat; 907 mg Sodium; 44 g Protein; 44 g Carbohydrate; 4 g Dietary Fiber

Take this to the next potluck. Good for a barbecue too.

Lean ground beef	1 lb.	454 g
Chopped onion	1½ cups	375 mL
Cooking oil	2 tsp.	10 mL
Canned kidney beans, drained	14 oz.	398 mL
Canned beans in tomato sauce	2 × 14 oz.	2 × 398 mL
Canned chick peas (garbanzo beans), drained	19 oz.	540 mL
Hickory smoked barbecue sauce	½ cup	125 mL
Brown sugar, packed	¼ cup	60 mL
White vinegar	1 tbsp.	15 mL
Prepared mustard	2 tsp.	10 mL
Salt	½ tsp.	2 mL
Pepper	⅛ tsp.	0.5 mL

Scramble-fry ground beef and onion in cooking oil in large frying pan until onion is soft and beef is no longer pink. Drain. Turn into ungreased 3 quart (3 L) casserole.

Add next 3 ingredients.

Stir remaining 6 ingredients together in small bowl. Add to casserole. Stir together lightly. Cover. Bake in 350°F (175°C) oven for about 1 hour until bubbling and browning around edge, stirring at half-time. Makes about 10 cups (2.5 L).

1½ cups (375 mL): 399 Calories; 9.2 g Total Fat; 1092 mg Sodium; 25 g Protein; 58 g Carbohydrate; 16 g Dietary Fiber

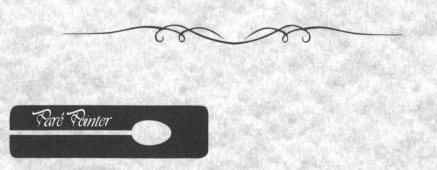

Paré Pointer

Sign over teller's window: Deposits welcomed, withdrawals tolerated.

DILLY BEEF DINNER

A slow cooker is required for this recipe. Long slow cooking tenderizes steak. A touch of dill adds to the flavor of this full meal.

Diced potato (about ½ inch, 12 mm)	4 cups	1 L
Thinly sliced carrot	3 cups	750 mL
Thinly sliced celery	¾ cup	175 mL
Sliced or chopped onion	1½ cups	375 mL
Beef flank steak (or brisket), cut into 6 serving pieces	2 lbs.	900 g
Canned tomatoes, with juice, broken up	14 oz.	398 mL
Dill weed	1½ tsp.	7 mL
Salt	1 tsp.	5 mL
Pepper	¼ tsp.	1 mL

Place potato, carrot, celery and onion in 5 quart (5 L) slow cooker.

Lay steak pieces over top.

Stir remaining 4 ingredients together in small bowl. Pour over beef. Cover. Cook on Low for 12 to 14 hours or on High for 6 to 7 hours. Serves 6.

1 serving: 324 Calories; 13.7 g Total Fat; 695 mg Sodium; 36 g Protein; 32 g Carbohydrate; 5 g Dietary Fiber

BEEFY RICE CASSEROLE

A slow cooker is required for this recipe. A mild chili flavor. Good mixture.

Cooking oil	1 tsp.	5 mL
Lean ground beef	1½ lbs.	680 g
Canned tomatoes, with juice	28 oz.	796 mL
Chopped onion	1½ cups	375 mL
Chopped green pepper	¼ cup	60 mL
Uncooked converted long grain rice	1 cup	250 mL
Salt	1½ tsp.	7 mL
Chili powder	1 tsp.	5 mL
Water	1 cup	250 mL

(continued on next page)

Heat cooking oil in medium non-stick frying pan. Add ground beef. Scramble-fry until beef is no longer pink. Drain. Turn into 3½ quart (3.5 L) slow cooker.

Add remaining 7 ingredients. Stir together. Cover. Cook on Low for 6 to 8 hours or on High for 3 to 4 hours. Makes 7½ cups (1.8 L).

1½ cups (375 mL): 414 Calories; 13 g Total Fat; 1138 mg Sodium; 29 g Protein; 44 g Carbohydrate; 3 g Dietary Fiber

VEGGIE BEEF CASSEROLE

Mild tomato flavor. Good creamy sauce.

Diced bacon	1 cup	250 mL
Lean ground beef	1½ lbs.	680 g
Medium onions, chopped	2	2
Thinly sliced potato	1½ cups	375 mL
Thinly sliced carrot	1½ cups	375 mL
Thinly sliced celery	½ cup	125 mL
Thinly sliced zucchini, with peel	1 cup	250 mL
Frozen cut green beans	1½ cups	375 mL
Uncooked broad noodles (about 6 oz., 170 g)	3 cups	750 mL
Salt	½ tsp.	2 mL
Condensed cream of mushroom soup	2 × 10 oz.	2 × 284 mL
Water	½ cup	125 mL
Condensed tomato soup	2 × 10 oz.	2 × 284 mL

Scramble-fry bacon, ground beef and onion in large frying pan until onion is soft and beef is no longer pink. Drain. Turn into ungreased 4 quart (4 L) casserole or small roaster.

Add next 7 ingredients. Stir together.

Stir mushroom soup and water together in small bowl. Add to beef mixture. Stir.

Empty tomato soup into small bowl. Stir vigorously. Spoon over all. Make sure pasta is underneath soup. Cover. Bake in 350°F (175°C) oven for 1½ to 2 hours until vegetables are tender. Serves 8.

1 serving: 436 Calories; 20.5 g Total Fat; 1558 mg Sodium; 25 g Protein; 38 g Carbohydrate; 3 g Dietary Fiber

STOVE TOP POT PIE

This not only tastes wonderful, it has a cozy look to it. Biscuit topping cooks on the top of the stove, not in the oven.

Medium carrots, cut into ¼ inch (6 mm) slices	4	4
Medium potatoes, cut into 1 inch (2.5 cm) cubes	4	4
Medium onion, cut into wedges	1	1
Large celery rib, coarsely chopped	1	1
Sliced fresh mushrooms	1 cup	250 mL
Diced zucchini, with peel	1 cup	250 mL
Boiling water	2 cups	500 mL
Canned stewed tomatoes, with juice, processed in blender	14 oz.	398 mL
Beef bouillon powder	2 tbsp.	30 mL
Worcestershire sauce	1 tsp.	5 mL
Pepper	⅛ tsp.	0.5 mL
Cooked roast beef, cut into ½ inch (12 mm) cubes	2 cups	500 mL
Instant potato flakes	2 tbsp.	30 mL
BISCUIT TOPPING		
Biscuit mix	1½ cups	375 mL
Milk	⅓ cup	75 mL

Combine first 11 ingredients in large pot or Dutch oven. Stir. Cover. Simmer for about 20 minutes until carrots are tender-crisp.

Add beef and potato flakes. Cook until hot and simmering.

Biscuit Topping: Stir biscuit mix and milk together in medium bowl to form soft ball. Knead on lightly floured surface 6 to 8 times. Roll out into ½ inch (12 mm) thick circle. Cut into 6 wedges. Position wedges on top of casserole. Cover. Cook for 12 to 15 minutes until biscuit wedges have risen and are cooked. Serves 6.

1 serving: 361 Calories; 7.7 g Total Fat; 1297 mg Sodium; 21 g Protein; 52 g Carbohydrate; 5 g Dietary Fiber

Pictured on page 17.

Meatballs, vegetables and beans. It's all here.

Large egg, fork-beaten	1	1
Dry bread crumbs	⅓ cup	75 mL
Finely minced onion	¼ cup	60 mL
Parsley flakes	1 tbsp.	15 mL
Seasoning salt	1 tsp.	5 mL
Lean ground beef	1 lb.	454 g
Cooking oil	2 tsp.	10 mL
Medium onion, halved and sliced	1	1
Medium green pepper, slivered	1	1
Canned diced tomatoes, with juice	19 oz.	540 mL
Medium carrot, grated	1	1
Granulated sugar	½ tsp.	2 mL
Dried whole oregano	¼ tsp.	1 mL
Dried sweet basil	¼ tsp.	1 mL
Bay leaf	1	1
Canned red kidney beans, drained	14 oz.	398 mL
Canned white kidney beans, drained	19 oz.	540 mL
Romano (or black) beans, drained	14 oz.	398 mL
Grated medium Cheddar cheese	¾ cup	175 mL

Stir first 5 ingredients together in medium bowl.

Add ground beef. Mix. Shape into 1 inch (2.5 cm) balls. You should get about 40.

Heat cooking oil in large pot or Dutch oven. Add meatballs. Cook until browned, removing to paper towel-lined plate as they brown. Drain all but 1 tsp. (5 mL) fat from pot.

Add onion and green pepper to pot. Sauté until onion is soft.

Add next 9 ingredients. Stir together. Add meatballs. Stir together gently. Simmer, uncovered, for about 30 minutes. Discard bay leaf.

Sprinkle cheese over each serving. Serves 6.

1 serving: 418 Calories; 14.1 g Total Fat; 844 mg Sodium; 31 g Protein; 43 g Carbohydrate; 8 g Dietary Fiber

BEEF STEWED IN WINE

Good hearty flavor. Full-bodied with a hint of bacon.

Bacon slices	4	4
All-purpose flour	3 tbsp.	50 mL
Salt	³/₄ tsp.	4 mL
Pepper	¹/₂ tsp.	2 mL
Garlic powder	¹/₂ tsp.	2 mL
Beef top round steak, trimmed of fat, cut into 1 inch (2.5 cm) cubes	2 lbs.	900 g
Large onion, sliced	1	1
Small (or medium, halved) fresh mushrooms	¹/₂ lb.	225 g
Sliced carrot	2 cups	500 mL
Dry red (or alcohol-free red) wine	¹/₄ cup	60 mL
Dry red (or alcohol-free red) wine	³/₄ cup	175 mL
Condensed beef broth	10 oz.	284 mL
Water	1 cup	250 mL
Bay leaves	2	2
Uncooked medium egg noodles	3 cups	750 mL

Cook bacon in large frying pan until browned. Remove to plate. Cut into 1 inch (2.5 cm) pieces. Drain all but 1 tbsp. (15 mL) fat from pan.

Combine flour, salt, pepper and garlic powder in bag or small bowl.

Add steak cubes, a few at a time, and shake to coat. Brown well in reserved bacon drippings in same frying pan, removing cubes to medium bowl as they brown. You will need to do this in 2 batches.

Add onion, mushrooms, carrot and first amount of wine to same frying pan. Stir to loosen any browned bits in pan. Return beef to pan.

Add second amount of wine, beef broth, water and bay leaves. Cover. Simmer for about 1¹/₂ hours until beef is very tender. Discard bay leaves.

Add noodles. Stir together. Noodles must be covered completely with vegetables or liquid. Cover. Boil gently for about 15 minutes until noodles are tender but firm. Add bacon. Stir together. Serves 6.

1 serving: 380 Calories; 11.3 g Total Fat; 788 mg Sodium; 35 g Protein; 26 g Carbohydrate; 3 g Dietary Fiber

Just place this in the oven before doing errands and see the incredible meal that awaits you when you get home.

Beef stew meat, cut into ¾ inch (2 cm) cubes	**1½ lbs.**	**680 g**
Cooking oil	**1 tsp.**	**5 mL**
Medium potatoes, cut up	**4**	**4**
Medium carrots, cut up	**5**	**5**
Medium onions, cut up	**2**	**2**
Sliced celery	**1 cup**	**250 mL**
Diced yellow turnip (rutabaga)	**1½ cups**	**375 mL**
Condensed onion soup	**10 oz.**	**284 mL**
Condensed tomato soup	**10 oz.**	**284 mL**
Salt	**½ tsp.**	**2 mL**
Pepper	**⅛ tsp.**	**0.5 mL**

Brown beef in cooking oil in large frying pan. Turn into small roaster.

Add next 5 ingredients.

Pour both soups, salt and pepper into same frying pan. Stir together well to loosen all browned bits in pan. Pour over vegetables. Cover. Bake in 300°F (150°C) oven for 3½ to 4 hours until tender. Makes 9 cups (2.25 L).

1½ cups (375 mL): 371 Calories; 12.3 g Total Fat; 1136 mg Sodium; 30 g Protein; 36 g Carbohydrate; 5 g Dietary Fiber

Politicians love ribbons, especially red tape.

BORSCHT STEW

Rich looking with a delicious beet flavor.

Boneless beef short ribs	2¹/₂ lbs.	1.1 kg
Sliced carrot	2 cups	500 mL
Sliced onion	1 cup	250 mL
Sliced celery	1 cup	250 mL
Tomato sauce	3 × 7¹/₂ oz.	3 × 213 mL
Water	1 cup	250 mL
Beef bouillon powder	2 tsp.	10 mL
Salt	2 tsp.	10 mL
Pepper	¹/₄ tsp.	1 mL
Dill weed	¹/₂ tsp.	2 mL
White vinegar	1 tbsp.	15 mL
Granulated sugar	2 tsp.	10 mL
Shredded cabbage	5 cups	1.25 L
Medium beets, peeled and cut into ¹/₄ inch (6 mm) thick matchsticks	3	3

Place ribs on rack in broiling tray. Broil each side for about 5 minutes until browned. Place in small roaster.

Add carrot, onion and celery.

Combine next 6 ingredients in medium bowl. Stir together. Pour over all. Cover. Bake in 325°F (160°C) oven for 2¹/₂ hours. Tilt roaster to skim off fat. Blot remaining fat with paper toweling.

Stir vinegar and sugar together in small cup. Pour over beef and vegetables.

Add cabbage and beets. Stir together as much as you can. Cover. Bake for about 1 hour until all vegetables and beef are tender. Serves 6.

1 serving: 440 Calories; 19.9 g Total Fat; 1987 mg Sodium; 42 g Protein; 24 g Carbohydrate; 4 g Dietary Fiber

Pictured on page 71.

A good beef and gravy dish with light, fluffy dumplings.

Beef stew meat, cut into ¾ inch (2 cm) cubes	1½ lbs.	680 g
Sliced onion	1 cup	250 mL
Beef bouillon powder	2 tsp.	10 mL
Salt	1 tsp.	5 mL
Pepper	¼ tsp.	1 mL
Water	1½ cups	375 mL
Water	¼ cup	60 mL
All-purpose flour	2 tbsp.	30 mL
Frozen peas (about 10 oz., 285 g)	2 cups	500 mL

BISCUIT DUMPLINGS

All-purpose flour	2 cups	500 mL
Baking powder	4 tsp.	20 mL
Granulated sugar	1 tbsp.	15 mL
Salt	¾ tsp.	4 mL
Cooking oil	⅓ cup	75 mL
Milk	¾ cup	175 mL
Hard margarine (or butter), melted (optional)	2 tsp.	10 mL

Put first 6 ingredients into ungreased 2 quart (2 L) casserole. Cover. Bake in 325°F (160°C) oven for about 3 hours, stirring each hour until beef is very tender. Remove from oven.

Whisk second amount of water and flour together in small bowl until smooth. Stir into casserole. Add peas. Stir. Cover to keep hot. Increase oven temperature to 400°F (205°C).

Biscuit Dumplings: Stir flour, baking powder, sugar and salt together in medium bowl.

Add cooking oil and milk. Stir together to make a ball. Knead on lightly floured surface 6 to 8 times. Roll out or press ¾ inch (2 cm) thick. Cut into 2 inch (5 cm) rounds. Arrange over top of beef mixture. Bake, uncovered, for about 20 minutes until lightly browned.

Brush hot dumplings with margarine. Serves 6.

1 serving: 551 Calories; 23.6 g Total Fat; 1139 mg Sodium; 33 g Protein; 50 g Carbohydrate; 4 g Dietary Fiber

Pictured on page 71.

POT ROAST

A sure way to get tender beef. A bit of nostalgia here. Makes lots of gravy.

Cooking oil	1 tsp.	5 mL
Boneless beef chuck (or blade or eye of round) roast	3 lbs.	1.4 kg
Boiling water	½ cup	125 mL
Beef bouillon powder	2 tsp.	10 mL
Canned tomatoes, with juice	14 oz.	398 mL
Brown sugar, packed	2 tbsp.	30 mL
Ground thyme	¼ tsp.	1 mL
Worcestershire sauce	1 tsp.	5 mL
Bay leaf	1	1
Medium potatoes, cut bite size	5	5
Medium carrots, cut bite size	6	6
Medium onions, cut into wedges	2	2
Salt	1 tsp.	5 mL
Pepper	¼ tsp.	1 mL
GRAVY		
All-purpose flour	¼ cup	60 mL
Water	½ cup	125 mL
Liquid gravy browner (optional)		
Salt, sprinkle (optional)		
Pepper, sprinkle (optional)		

Heat cooking oil in heavy pot or Dutch oven. Add roast. Brown both sides.

Stir boiling water and bouillon powder together in small cup. Add to beef.

Add next 5 ingredients. Stir around beef. Bring to a boil. Cover. Simmer gently for about 2½ hours until beef is tender. Turn beef 2 or 3 times while cooking. Add more liquid if needed to keep 1½ to 2 inches (3.8 to 5 cm) deep.

Add potato, carrot, onion, salt and pepper around beef. Cover. Simmer for 30 to 40 minutes until vegetables are tender. Discard bay leaf. Strain juice into measuring cup. Add water, if necessary, to make 2 cups (500 mL).

(continued on next page)

Gravy: Pour juice into small saucepan. Skim off fat. Mix flour and water in small cup until no lumps remain. Gradually add flour mixture until boiling and thickened. Add a bit of gravy browner for color. Taste for salt and pepper, adding if needed. Makes 3½ cups (875 mL). Serves 6.

1 serving: 497 Calories; 14.3 g Total Fat; 992 mg Sodium; 51 g Protein; 40 g Carbohydrate; 5 g Dietary Fiber

DINTY'S SPECIAL

Mild, satisfying and easy to make.

Shredded cabbage	4 cups	1 L
Chopped onion	½ cup	125 mL
Water	1½ cups	375 mL
Canned corned beef, cut into ½ inch (12 mm) cubes	12 oz.	340 g
Diced medium Cheddar cheese	1 cup	250 mL
Milk	1½ cups	375 mL
All-purpose flour	3 tbsp.	50 mL
Salt	½ tsp.	2 mL
Pepper	⅛ tsp.	0.5 mL
Jar of chopped pimiento, drained	2 oz.	57 mL
TOPPING		
Hard margarine (or butter)	¼ cup	60 mL
Dry bread crumbs	1 cup	250 mL

Cook cabbage and onion in water in large saucepan until tender. Drain. Turn into ungreased 2 quart (2 L) casserole. Cool.

Add corned beef and cheese. Stir together.

Gradually whisk milk into flour in small saucepan until no lumps remain. Heat and stir until boiling and thickened. Stir in salt, pepper and pimiento. Pour into casserole. Stir.

Topping: Melt margarine in small saucepan. Stir in bread crumbs. Sprinkle over top. Bake, uncovered, in 350°F (175°C) oven for about 30 minutes. Serves 6.

1 serving: 431 Calories; 25 g Total Fat; 1200 mg Sodium; 26 g Protein; 25 g Carbohydrate; 2 g Dietary Fiber

STEAK IN FOIL

An autumn mix of colors. Cooking in foil means no pan to wash.

Beef chuck steak	1½ lbs.	680 g
Envelope dry onion soup mix	1 x 1½ oz.	1 x 42 g
Condensed cream of mushroom soup	10 oz.	284 mL
Medium sweet potatoes (size of medium potatoes)	4	4
Medium parsnips, quartered	4	4
Medium onions, quartered	2	2

Place large piece of foil in small roaster, leaving ends hanging outside roaster. Lay steak on foil.

Combine dry soup mix and mushroom soup in small bowl. Spread over beef.

Arrange sweet potatoes, parsnip and onion over top. Fold foil and seal. Cover. Bake in 300°F (150°C) oven for 2½ to 3 hours. Carefully open foil to test for doneness with fork. Steak should be very tender. Serves 4.

1 serving: 530 Calories; 16.7 g Total Fat; 1712 mg Sodium; 40 g Protein; 55 g Carbohydrate; 8 g Dietary Fiber

Variation: Omit sweet potatoes and parsnips. Add potatoes and carrots.

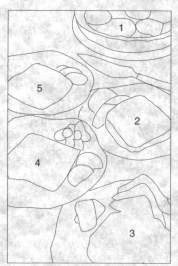

1. Red-Topped Frittata, page 41
2. Ham Stratawich, page 42
3. Egg Scramble Deluxe, page 44
4. Zucchini Frittata, page 40
5. Breakfast Strata, page 45

Props Courtesy Of: C C on Whyte, Dansk Gifts, Eaton's, Handworks Gallery, Stokes, The Bay

A tendor and juicy dinner.

Beef short ribs, cut up	3½ lbs.	1.6 kg
White vinegar	3 tbsp.	50 mL
Brown sugar, packed	3 tbsp.	50 mL
Salt	1½ tsp.	7 mL
Pepper	½ tsp.	2 mL
Beef bouillon powder	2 tsp.	10 mL
Garlic powder	¼ tsp.	1 mL
Prepared horseradish	1 tbsp.	15 mL
Water, to cover		
Medium potatoes, quartered	4	4
Sliced onion	1 cup	250 mL
Peeled baby carrots	24	24
GRAVY		
All-purpose flour	¼ cup	60 mL
Salt	½ tsp.	2 mL
Liquid gravy browner (optional)		

Place ribs on rack in broiling tray. Broil each side for 5 minutes until browned. Place in small roaster.

Mix next 7 ingredients in small bowl. Pour over short ribs.

Add enough water to barely cover beef. Cover. Bake in 325°F (160°C) oven for 1½ to 2 hours until almost tender.

Add potato, onion and carrots. Cover. Bake for 1 hour until beef is very tender and vegetables are cooked. Strain liquid into measuring cup. Add water to make 2 cups (500 mL).

Gravy: Gradually whisk strained liquid into flour and salt in small saucepan until smooth. Heat and stir until boiling and thickened. Add bit of gravy browner for color. Makes 2 cups (500 mL). Serves 4.

1 serving: 920 Calories; 41.1 g Total Fat; 1999 mg Sodium; 84 g Protein; 50 g Carbohydrate; 5 g Dietary Fiber

CORNY BEEF ENCHILADAS

You can make these as spicy as you like by adjusting the kind of salsa you use as well as adding jalapeño peppers.

Chopped cooked roast beef	2 cups	500 mL
Cooked kernel corn	1 cup	250 mL
Canned chopped green chilies, drained	4 oz.	114 mL
Mild or medium salsa	2/3 cup	150 mL
Ground cumin	1/2 tsp.	2 mL
Salt	1/2 tsp.	2 mL
Mild or medium salsa	2/3 cup	150 mL
Corn tortillas (6 inches, 15 cm)	8	8
Mild or medium salsa	2/3 cup	150 mL
Grated sharp Cheddar cheese	1 cup	250 mL
Chopped pitted ripe olives (optional)	2 tbsp.	30 mL
Chopped jalapeño peppers (optional)	2 tbsp.	30 mL

Combine first 6 ingredients in medium bowl.

Spread second amount of salsa in greased casserole large enough to hold 8 enchiladas in single layer.

Place 1 tortilla on working surface. Cover remaining tortillas with damp tea towel to keep from drying out. Place about 1/3 cup (75 mL) beef mixture on tortilla. Fold sides over center. Lay, folded side up, over salsa in casserole. Repeat with remaining tortillas.

Drizzle third amount of salsa over enchiladas. Sprinkle with cheese, olives and jalapeño peppers. Cover. Bake in 350°F (175°C) oven for 45 minutes. Remove cover. Bake for about 15 minutes until very hot. Makes 8 enchiladas. Serves 4.

1 serving: 529 Calories; 16.7 g Total Fat; 2665 mg Sodium; 38 g Protein; 62 g Carbohydrate; 6 g Dietary Fiber

Variation: Scramble-fry 1 lb. (454 g) lean ground beef to use instead of roast beef.

CORNED BEEF BAKE

Taste of corned beef comes through. Mellow and flavorful.

Chopped onion	½ cup	125 mL
Cooking oil	1 tsp.	5 mL
Canned corned beef, cut into ½ inch (12 mm) cubes	12 oz.	340 g
Frozen peas	2 cups	500 mL
Fettuccine, broken up	8 oz.	225 g
Boiling water	3 qts.	3 L
Cooking oil (optional)	1 tbsp.	15 mL
Salt	2 tsp.	10 mL
Condensed cream of mushroom soup	10 oz.	284 mL
Milk	¼ cup	60 mL
TOPPING		
Hard margarine (or butter)	2 tbsp.	30 mL
Soda cracker crumbs	½ cup	125 mL

Sauté onion in first amount of cooking oil in small frying pan until soft. Turn into ungreased 2½ quart (2.5 L) casserole.

Add corned beef and peas. Stir together.

Cook pasta in boiling water, second amount of cooking oil and salt in large uncovered pot or Dutch oven for 5 to 7 minutes, stirring occasionally, until tender but firm. Drain. Add to casserole. Stir as best you can.

Mix soup and milk in small bowl. Pour over casserole. Poke with knife in several places to allow soup to run through.

Topping: Melt margarine in small saucepan. Stir in cracker crumbs. Sprinkle over top. Bake, uncovered, in 350°F (175°C) oven for 20 to 30 minutes until bubbly hot. Serves 6.

1 serving: 451 Calories; 18.7 g Total Fat; 1157 mg Sodium; 25 g Protein; 45 g Carbohydrate; 4 g Dietary Fiber

ZUCCHINI FRITTATA

Zucchini fits right into this tasty concoction.

Cooking oil	1 tbsp.	15 mL
Medium onion, chopped	1	1
Medium potato, diced small	1	1
Medium zucchini, with peel, thinly sliced	2	2
Large eggs	8	8
Grated Parmesan cheese	2¹/₂ tbsp.	37 mL
Salt	¹/₂ tsp.	2 mL
Dried sweet basil, sprinkle		
Dried whole oregano, sprinkle		
Pepper, sprinkle		
Grated medium Cheddar cheese	¹/₂ cup	125 mL

Heat cooking oil in large non-stick frying pan. Add onion, potato and zucchini. Sauté until potato is almost cooked and onion and zucchini are soft.

Beat eggs in medium bowl until smooth. Add next 5 ingredients. Beat together well. Pour over zucchini mixture. Cover. Cook over medium-low for 13 to 15 minutes until eggs are set.

Remove from heat. Sprinkle with Cheddar cheese. Cover. Let stand for 2 to 4 minutes until cheese is melted. Serves 4.

1 serving: 299 Calories; 19.6 g Total Fat; 622 mg Sodium; 19 g Protein; 12 g Carbohydrate; 2 g Dietary Fiber

Note: Stove top temperatures may affect cooking time. If cooked too low, top eggs won't set. If cooked too high, bottom eggs burn.

Pictured on page 35.

Paré Pointer

They are trying their best to budget so that they can live beyond their yearnings.

RED-TOPPED FRITTATA

Tomatoes nesting in a poofy egg pie. Serve at your next brunch.

Hard margarine (or butter)	2 tsp.	10 mL
Chopped onion	½ cup	125 mL
Diced green, red or yellow pepper	⅓ cup	75 mL
Chopped cooked ham (5 oz., 140 g)	1 cup	250 mL
Grated Edam (or Gouda) cheese	½ cup	125 mL
Large eggs, fork-beaten	6	6
Salt	1 tsp.	5 mL
Pepper, sprinkle		
Cayenne pepper, sprinkle		
Medium tomatoes, sliced	2	2

Heat margarine in large frying pan. Add onion. Sauté until onion is beginning to soften.

Add green pepper and ham. Sauté for 2 to 3 minutes. Turn into greased 10 inch (25 cm) glass pie plate or shallow 9 × 9 inch (22 × 22 cm) casserole.

Sprinkle with cheese.

Stir eggs, salt, pepper and cayenne pepper together in medium bowl. Pour over cheese.

Arrange tomato slices over top, overlapping if necessary. Bake, uncovered, in 350°F (175°C) oven for about 30 minutes until set. Serves 4.

1 serving: 289 Calories; 20.4 g Total Fat; 1422 mg Sodium; 20 g Protein; 7 g Carbohydrate; 1 g Dietary Fiber

Pictured on page 35.

Sergeants in the army must suffer from headaches. They are always shouting "Tension."

HAM STRATAWICH

Very tasty and very showy with an evenly browned top. A handy make-ahead breakfast or brunch. Cuts nicely into "sandwiches."

Sliced onion	1 cup	250 mL
Cooking oil	1 tsp.	5 mL
Bread slices, with crusts	6	6
Frozen chopped broccoli, thawed (chop larger pieces smaller)	2½ cups	625 mL
Diced cooked ham	2 cups	500 mL
Grated medium Cheddar cheese	2 cups	500 mL
Bread slices, with crusts	6	6
Large eggs	5	5
Milk	2½ cups	625 mL
Dry mustard	½ tsp.	2 mL
Salt	½ tsp.	2 mL
Pepper	¼ tsp.	1 mL
Garlic powder	¼ tsp.	1 mL
Onion powder	¼ tsp.	1 mL
TOPPING		
Hard margarine (or butter)	2 tbsp.	30 mL
Coarsely crushed corn flakes cereal	½ cup	125 mL

Sauté onion in cooking oil in medium frying pan until soft.

Line greased 9 × 13 inch (22 × 33 cm) pan with first amount of bread slices. Spread onion over top. Layer with broccoli, ham, cheese and second amount of bread slices.

Beat eggs in medium bowl until smooth. Add next 6 ingredients. Mix. Pour over all.

Topping: Melt margarine in small saucepan. Stir in corn flake crumbs. Sprinkle over egg mixture. Cover. Refrigerate overnight. Remove cover. Bake in 325°F (160°C) oven for about 1 hour. Serves 6.

1 serving: 612 Calories; 30.6 g Total Fat; 1666 mg Sodium; 35 g Protein; 49 g Carbohydrate; 4 g Dietary Fiber

Pictured on page 35.

Nicely browned. Attractive and good flavor combination.

Pastry (your own or a mix), for 10 inch (25 cm) pie		
Frozen chopped spinach, thawed and squeezed dry	10 oz.	300 g
Canned french-fried onions	¹/₂ × 2³/₄ oz.	¹/₂ × 79 g
Crumbled feta cheese	1¹/₂ cups	375 mL
Grated sharp Cheddar cheese	²/₃ cup	150 mL
Large eggs	4	4
Skim evaporated milk	13¹/₂ oz.	385 mL
Pepper	¹/₄ tsp.	1 mL
Ground nutmeg	¹/₁₆ tsp.	0.5 mL
Canned french-fried onions	¹/₂ × 2³/₄ oz.	¹/₂ × 79 g
Parsley flakes	1 tsp.	5 mL

Roll out pastry on lightly floured surface. Fit into ungreased 10 inch (25 cm) glass pie plate. Glass will ensure a browned bottom crust. Trim and crimp edge.

Scatter spinach in pie shell. Sprinkle first amount of onion rings over spinach. Sprinkle with both cheeses.

Beat eggs in medium bowl until smooth. Add next 3 ingredients. Beat together. Pour over cheese.

Scatter second amount of onion rings and parsley over top. Bake, uncovered, on bottom rack in 375°F (190°C) oven for about 45 minutes until knife inserted in center comes out clean. Let stand for 5 to 10 minutes before cutting. Cuts into 8 wedges.

1 wedge: 341 Calories; 21.2 g Total Fat; 666 mg Sodium; 16 g Protein; 22 g Carbohydrate; 1 g Dietary Fiber

Pictured on page 71.

Paré Pointer

She thought a filling station was a dentist's office.

EGG SCRAMBLE DELUXE

A fast and easy dish to prepare for the whole family.

Large eggs	8	8
Water	3 tbsp.	50 mL
Grated sharp Cheddar cheese	½ cup	125 mL
Worcestershire sauce	¼ tsp.	1 mL
Canned flakes of ham, with liquid, broken up	6½ oz.	184 g
Salt, sprinkle		
Pepper, sprinkle		
Hard margarine (or butter)	1 tsp.	5 mL

Beat eggs and water together in medium bowl.

Add cheese, Worcestershire sauce, ham flakes with liquid, salt and pepper. Stir together well.

Melt margarine in large non-stick frying pan. Add egg mixture. Scramble-fry constantly until softly set. Serves 8.

1 serving: 164 Calories; 12.3 g Total Fat; 431 mg Sodium; 12 g Protein; 1 g Carbohydrate; 0 g Dietary Fiber

Pictured on page 35.

Phantoms always pick up their mail at the ghost office.

Sausage always adds a good taste to anything for breakfast as it does in this strata. A great make-ahead.

Bread slices, crusts removed	8	8
Grated medium Cheddar cheese	2 cups	500 mL
Small pork sausages, browned and each cut into 4 or 5 pieces	1½ lbs.	680 g
Large eggs	5	5
Milk	2¼ cups	560 mL
Dry mustard	½ tsp.	2 mL
Onion salt	¼ tsp.	1 mL
Pepper	⅛ tsp.	0.5 mL
Condensed cream of mushroom soup	10 oz.	284 mL
Milk	½ cup	125 mL
TOPPING		
Hard margarine (or butter)	2 tbsp.	30 mL
Dry bread crumbs	½ cup	125 mL

Line greased 9 x 13 inch (22 x 33 cm) pan with bread slices, trimming to fit. Sprinkle with cheese. Scatter sausage over cheese.

Beat eggs in medium bowl until smooth. Add next 4 ingredients. Stir together. Pour over sausage. Cover. Refrigerate overnight.

About 45 minutes before serving, mix soup and second amount of milk in small bowl. Pour over all. Let stand for 30 to 45 minutes.

Topping: Melt margarine in small saucepan. Stir in bread crumbs. Sprinkle over top. Bake, uncovered, in 350°F (175°C) oven for about 1½ hours. Let stand for 10 to 15 minutes before serving. Serves 8.

1 serving: 521 Calories; 33.5 g Total Fat; 1365 mg Sodium; 26 g Protein; 28 g Carbohydrate; 1 g Dietary Fiber

Pictured on page 35.

Paré Pointer

They call their kitten "Penny" because it has a head on one side and a tail on the other.

TUNA FRILLS

Perky little rolls filled with tuna, spinach and different kinds of cheese.

Lasagne noodles	8	8
Boiling water	3 qts.	3 L
Cooking oil (optional)	1 tbsp.	15 mL
Salt	2 tsp.	10 mL
SAUCE		
Hard margarine (or butter)	1 tbsp.	15 mL
Medium onion, finely chopped	1	1
All-purpose flour	1 tbsp.	15 mL
Chicken bouillon powder	1 tsp.	5 mL
Garlic salt	1/2 tsp.	2 mL
Dill weed	1/2 tsp.	2 mL
Dry mustard	1/2 tsp.	2 mL
Cayenne pepper, sprinkle		
Milk	2 cups	500 mL
Canned flaked tuna, drained	6 oz.	170 g
Large egg, fork-beaten	1	1
Part-skim ricotta cheese	16 oz.	500 g
Frozen chopped spinach, thawed	10 oz.	300 g
and squeezed dry		
Grated part-skim mozzarella cheese	1 cup	250 mL
Grated Parmesan cheese	1/3 cup	75 mL
Parsley flakes	1 tbsp.	15 mL
Dried sweet basil	1 tsp.	5 mL
Garlic salt	1/2 tsp.	2 mL
Pepper	1/4 tsp.	1 mL

Fresh dill, sprinkle (optional)

Cook pasta in boiling water, cooking oil and salt in large uncovered pot or Dutch oven for 10 to 12 minutes, stirring occasionally, until tender but firm. Drain. Rinse with cold water. Drain.

Sauce: Melt margarine in large frying pan. Add onion. Sauté until soft.

Mix in next 6 ingredients. Stir in milk until boiling and thickened.

Add tuna. Mix well. Pour 1/2 of sauce into greased 9 x 9 inch (22 x 22 cm) pan or casserole.

(continued on next page)

Combine next 9 ingredients in medium bowl. Spread about ½ cup (125 mL) spinach mixture down length of each noodle. Roll up. Cut each roll in half crosswise. Set in pan, frill side up. Pour remaining ½ of sauce over and around noodles. Cover. Bake in 350°F (175°C) oven for 1 to 1½ hours until bubbly hot.

Garnish with dill. Makes 16 frills, enough for 4 large servings.

1 serving: 622 Calories; 24.9 g Total Fat; 1254 mg Sodium; 48 g Protein; 51 g Carbohydrate; 3 g Dietary Fiber

Pictured on page 17.

TUNA POTATO GRIDDLE

It takes many adjectives such as colorful, moist and perfectly seasoned to describe this meal. This is similar to fried onion and potato.

Hard margarine (or butter)	1 tbsp.	15 mL
Finely chopped onion	½ cup	125 mL
Diced green or red pepper	½ cup	125 mL
Frozen hash brown potatoes	4 cups	1 L
Seasoning salt	1 tsp.	5 mL
Pepper, sprinkle		
Frozen mixed vegetables	1 cup	250 mL
Canned flaked tuna, drained	6 oz.	170 g
Grated medium Cheddar cheese	1 cup	250 mL

Melt margarine in large frying pan. Add onion and green pepper. Sauté until onion is soft.

Add potatoes, seasoning salt and pepper. Stir together. Cover. Cook for about 5 minutes until potatoes are soft.

Stir in vegetables and tuna. Cover. Cook for about 5 minutes until hot.

Sprinkle with cheese. Cover. Let stand for 2 to 3 minutes until cheese is melted. Makes 5 cups (1.25 L).

1 cup (250 mL): 332 Calories; 12.2 g Total Fat; 611 mg Sodium; 19 g Protein; 39 g Carbohydrate; 5 g Dietary Fiber

STANDBY TUNA CASSEROLE

Can be prepared ahead of time and baked when needed. Delicious.

Small shell pasta	1 cup	250 mL
Boiling water	6 cups	1.5 L
Cooking oil (optional)	2 tsp.	10 mL
Salt	1 tsp.	5 mL
Chopped onion	½ cup	125 mL
Chopped red pepper	½ cup	125 mL
Hard margarine (or butter)	2 tsp.	10 mL
Chopped fresh mushrooms	1 cup	250 mL
All-purpose flour	2 tbsp.	30 mL
Skim evaporated milk	13½ oz.	385 mL
Beef bouillon powder	2 tsp.	10 mL
Celery seed	½ tsp.	2 mL
Pepper, sprinkle		
Light process Cheddar (or mozzarella) cheese slices	4	4
Canned solid white tuna, drained and broken into chunks	6½ oz.	184 g
Grated medium Cheddar cheese	½ cup	125 mL

Cook pasta in boiling water, cooking oil and salt in large uncovered saucepan for 8 to 10 minutes, stirring occasionally, until tender but firm. Drain. Return to saucepan.

Sauté onion and red pepper in margarine in separate large saucepan until onion is soft. Add mushrooms. Sauté until liquid is evaporated.

Whisk flour and evaporated milk together in small bowl until smooth. Add to onion mixture, stirring often, until boiling and thickened.

Add bouillon powder, celery seed, pepper and cheese slices. Stir until cheese is melted.

Add tuna and pasta. Stir. Pour into greased 2 quart (2 L) casserole.

Sprinkle with cheese. Bake, uncovered, in 350°F (175°C) oven for about 35 minutes. Serves 4.

1 serving: 375 Calories; 10.1 g Total Fat; 997 mg Sodium; 31 g Protein; 40 g Carbohydrate; 2 g Dietary Fiber

QUICK TUNA CASSEROLE

Kids will discover this in a hurry

Condensed cream of mushroom soup	10 oz.	284 mL
Milk	¾ cup	175 mL
Salt	½ tsp.	2 mL
Pepper	¼ tsp.	1 mL
Dried whole oregano (optional)	½ tsp.	2 mL
Uncooked instant white rice	2 cups	500 mL
Frozen peas and carrots	2 cups	500 mL
Onion flakes	1 tbsp.	15 mL
Canned solid white tuna, drained and flaked	6½ oz.	184 g
TOPPING		
Hard margarine (or butter)	2 tbsp.	30 mL
Dry bread crumbs	½ cup	125 mL

Mix first 5 ingredients in large bowl.

Add next 4 ingredients. Stir. Turn into ungreased 2 quart (2 L) casserole.

Topping: Melt margarine in small saucepan. Stir in bread crumbs. Sprinkle over top. Bake, uncovered, in 350°F (175°C) oven for about 30 minutes. Serves 4.

1 serving: 490 Calories; 14.1 g Total Fat; 1350 mg Sodium; 21 g Protein; 70 g Carbohydrate; 4 g Dietary Fiber

Paré Pointer

Tennis players have to be satisfied with net profits.

MUSHROOM AND CRAB CASSEROLE

Assemble ahead of time, cover and refrigerate. Bake when ready.

Sliced fresh mushrooms	2 cups	500 mL
White (or alcohol-free white) wine	1 tbsp.	15 mL
All-purpose flour	2 tbsp.	30 mL
Skim milk	2 cups	500 mL
Light spreadable cream cheese	2 tbsp.	30 mL
Canned crabmeat, drained and cartilage removed (or 2 cups, 500 mL, chopped imitation crabmeat)	2 x 4 oz.	2 x 113 g
Seafood (or vegetable) bouillon powder	$\frac{1}{2}$ tsp.	2 mL
Salt	$\frac{1}{2}$ tsp.	2 mL
Dried sweet basil	$\frac{1}{4}$ tsp.	1 mL
Cayenne pepper, sprinkle		
Freshly ground pepper, sprinkle		
Ground nutmeg, sprinkle		
Jar of sliced pimiento, drained (optional)	2 oz.	57 mL
Small shell pasta (about 8 oz., 225 g)	$2\frac{1}{3}$ cups	575 mL
Boiling water	2 qts.	2 L
Cooking oil (optional)	1 tbsp.	15 mL
Salt	2 tsp.	10 mL
Grated light Monterey Jack cheese	$\frac{1}{2}$ cup	125 mL
Grated light Parmesan cheese product	1 tbsp.	15 mL

Sauté mushrooms in large non-stick frying pan for 7 to 8 minutes until liquid is evaporated.

Add wine. Simmer for about 1 minute until liquid is almost evaporated.

Measure flour into small bowl. Gradually whisk in milk until smooth. Add to mushrooms, stirring constantly, until boiling and thickened. Stir in cream cheese until melted.

Stir in next 8 ingredients. Remove from heat.

(continued on next page)

Cook pasta in boiling water, cooking oil and second amount of salt in large uncovered pot or Dutch oven for 4 minutes, stirring occasionally. Pasta will still be slightly firm. Drain. Rinse with cold water. Drain. Add to crab sauce. Mix. Pour into greased 1½ quart (1.5 L) casserole.

Sprinkle with Monterey Jack cheese and Parmesan cheese. Cover. Bake in 350°F (175°C) oven for 30 minutes until hot and bubbling. Serves 4.

1 serving: 385 Calories; 5.8 g Total Fat; 1065 mg Sodium; 27 g Protein; 55 g Carbohydrate; 2 g Dietary Fiber

NEPTUNE'S PIE

If shepherds can have a pie, so can Neptune.

Medium potatoes, cut up (about 1½ lbs., 680 g)	6	6
Water, to cover		
Hot milk	⅔ cup	150 mL
Hard margarine (or butter)	2 tbsp.	30 mL
Salt	¼ tsp.	1 mL
Pepper	1/16 tsp.	0.5 mL
Fine dry bread crumbs	½ cup	125 mL
Salt	½ tsp.	2 mL
Onion powder	½ tsp.	2 mL
Poultry seasoning	¾ tsp.	4 mL
Fish fillets (your choice)	1¼ lbs.	568 g
Frozen peas and carrots	2 cups	500 mL
Paprika, sprinkle		

Cook potato in water in large saucepan until tender. Drain.

Add milk, margarine, first amount of salt and pepper. Mash together well. Keep warm.

Mix next 4 ingredients in small bowl.

Dip fish into crumb mixture to coat. Arrange in greased 9 x 9 inch (22 x 22 cm) pan. Spread peas and carrots over top. Spoon dabs of potato here and there. Smooth out as best you can. Sprinkle with paprika. Bake, uncovered, in 400°F (205°C) oven for 30 minutes. Serves 4.

1 serving: 415 Calories; 8.5 g Total Fat; 1107 mg Sodium; 34 g Protein; 51 g Carbohydrate; 5 g Dietary Fiber

Fish & Seafood   51

FISH FANTASTIC

Delicate, rich, tart, sweet and scrumptious.

Long grain white rice	¾ cup	175 mL
Water	1½ cups	375 mL
Salt	½ tsp.	2 mL
Condensed cream of mushroom soup	10 oz.	284 mL
Light salad dressing (or mayonnaise)	½ cup	125 mL
Milk	½ cup	125 mL
Lemon juice	1 tsp.	5 mL
Onion flakes	1 tbsp.	15 mL
Curry powder	½ tsp.	2 mL
Frozen chopped broccoli, thawed and drained	2¼ cups	560 mL
Fish fillets (your choice), cut bite size	1 lb.	454 g

Cook rice in water and salt in covered medium saucepan for 15 to 20 minutes until tender and water is absorbed. Transfer to ungreased 9 x 9 inch (22 x 22 cm) pan.

Mix next 6 ingredients in medium bowl until fairly smooth.

Add broccoli and fish. Stir lightly. Pour over rice. Cover. Bake in 350°F (175°C) oven for 30 to 40 minutes until fish flakes when tested with fork. Serves 4.

1 serving: 438 Calories; 15.3 g Total Fat; 1291 mg Sodium; 28 g Protein; 47 g Carbohydrate; 4 g Dietary Fiber

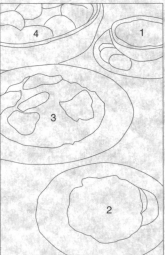

1. Minestrone, page 141
2. Macaroni Hash, page 12
3. Rice And Broccoli Chicken, page 111
4. Patty Bake, page 13

Cheesy with a hint of dill.

Hard margarine (or butter)	1 tbsp.	15 mL
Chopped onion	½ cup	125 mL
Chopped celery	1 cup	250 mL
Chopped green or red pepper	⅔ cup	150 mL
Uncooked converted long grain rice	1¼ cups	300 mL
Water	1½ cups	375 mL
Condensed Cheddar cheese soup	10 oz.	284 mL
Milk	⅔ cup	150 mL
Light cream cheese, cut up	4 oz.	125 g
Canned salmon, drained, skin and round bones removed, flaked	7½ oz.	213 g
Frozen baby peas, thawed	1 cup	250 mL
Chopped fresh dill (or ½ tsp., 2 mL, dill weed)	2 tsp.	10 mL

Melt margarine in large non-stick frying pan. Add onion, celery and green pepper. Sauté until soft.

Add rice, water, soup and milk. Stir together. Bring to a boil. Cover. Simmer for 30 to 40 minutes until rice is tender.

Add cream cheese. Stir until melted.

Add salmon and peas. Stir. Heat through.

Garnish with dill. Makes 8 cups (2 L).

1½ cups (375 mL): 412 Calories; 13.7 g Total Fat; 937 mg Sodium; 19 g Protein; 52 g Carbohydrate; 3 g Dietary Fiber

Paré Pointer

That fellow made a fortune from operating a flea circus. He started from scratch.

SCALLOPED SALMON

Fabulous fare for company as well as family. Red salmon is best for color.

Box of au gratin scalloped potatoes with sauce packet	5½ oz.	155 g
Water	2¼ cups	560 mL
Milk	1 cup	250 mL
Dill weed	¼ tsp.	1 mL
Onion salt	¼ tsp.	1 mL
Onion flakes	1 tbsp.	15 mL
Frozen peas	2 cups	500 mL
Canned salmon, drained, skin and round bones removed, flaked	7½ oz.	213 g
TOPPING		
Hard margarine (or butter)	2 tbsp.	30 mL
Dry bread crumbs	½ cup	125 mL

Combine potatoes and sauce packet in ungreased 2 quart (2 L) casserole.

Heat water, milk, dill weed and onion salt in medium saucepan until boiling. Pour over potatoes. Stir. Cover. Bake in 350°F (175°C) oven for 20 to 30 minutes until potato is tender.

Sprinkle with onion flakes. Scatter peas over onion flakes. Spread salmon over peas.

Topping: Melt margarine in small saucepan. Stir in bread crumbs. Sprinkle over all. Bake, uncovered, in 350°F (175°C) oven for about 30 minutes. Serves 4.

1 serving: 446 Calories; 18.5 g Total Fat; 1272 mg Sodium; 21 g Protein; 52 g Carbohydrate; 6 g Dietary Fiber

Pare Pointer

Those farm kids couldn't stand milking so they sat down.

A slow cooker is required for this recipe. A full meal with fish as the cornerstone rather than beef. Red salmon is best for color.

Medium potatoes, thinly sliced	4	4
Thinly sliced carrot	1 cup	250 mL
Chopped onion	1 cup	250 mL
All-purpose flour	2 tbsp.	30 mL
Salt	1 tsp.	5 mL
Pepper	1/8 tsp.	0.5 mL
Canned salmon, drained, skin and round bones removed, flaked	2 x 7 1/2 oz.	2 x 213 g
Condensed cream of mushroom soup	10 oz.	284 mL
Water	1/4 cup	60 mL
Parsley flakes	1/2 tsp.	2 mL
Paprika	1/4 tsp.	1 mL

Place first 6 ingredients in 5 quart (5 L) slow cooker. Stir together well to coat with flour.

Scatter salmon over top.

Stir remaining 4 ingredients together in small bowl. Pour over all. Cover. Cook on Low for 9 to 11 hours or on High for 4 1/2 to 5 1/2 hours. Makes 5 1/4 cups (1.3 L).

1 1/2 cups (375 mL): 407 Calories; 13.2 g Total Fat; 2051 mg Sodium; 30 g Protein; 42 g Carbohydrate; 4 g Dietary Fiber

Paré Pointer

That small piece of land is like a bad tooth. It's an acre.

SHRIMP SUPREME

A bit reminiscent of shrimp cocktail. Flavor is great.

Long grain white rice	1 cup	250 mL
Water	2 cups	500 mL
Salt	½ tsp.	2 mL
Cooking oil	1 tsp.	5 mL
Chopped onion	½ cup	125 mL
Finely chopped green pepper	¼ cup	60 mL
Chopped fresh mushrooms	1 cup	250 mL
Condensed tomato soup	10 oz.	284 mL
Skim evaporated milk	1 cup	250 mL
Salt	1 tsp.	5 mL
Pepper	¼ tsp.	1 mL
Ground nutmeg, just a pinch		
Sherry (or alcohol-free sherry)	3 tbsp.	50 mL
Worcestershire sauce	½ tsp.	2 mL
Cooked medium fresh (or frozen, thawed) shrimp	1 lb.	454 g
Lemon juice	1 tbsp.	15 mL
Sliced almonds, toasted	2 tbsp.	30 mL

Cook rice in water and first amount of salt in covered medium saucepan for 15 to 20 minutes until tender and water is absorbed. Transfer to ungreased 2 quart (2 L) casserole.

Heat cooking oil in medium frying pan. Add onion, green pepper and mushrooms. Sauté until soft. Add to rice. Stir.

Stir next 7 ingredients together well in medium bowl. Pour over rice mixture.

Put shrimp into medium bowl. Drain well. Blot dry with paper towels. Drizzle with lemon juice. Toss to coat. Let stand for 10 minutes. Add to casserole. Toss lightly to distribute shrimp evenly.

Sprinkle with almonds. Bake, uncovered, in 350°F (175°C) oven for 45 to 60 minutes until heated through. Let stand for 10 minutes before serving. Makes 8 cups (2 L).

1½ cups (375 mL): 335 Calories; 4.3 g Total Fat; 1414 mg Sodium; 26 g Protein; 46 g Carbohydrate; 2 g Dietary Fiber

Fresh or frozen shrimp give this a nice fresh taste.

Cooking oil	2 tsp.	10 mL
Chopped onion	1 cup	250 mL
Chopped celery	¾ cup	175 mL
Chopped green pepper	⅓ cup	75 mL
Fettuccine, broken	8 oz.	225 g
Boiling water	3 qts.	3 L
Cooking oil (optional)	1 tbsp.	15 mL
Salt	2 tsp.	10 mL
Condensed cream of mushroom soup	10 oz.	284 mL
Parsley flakes	2 tsp.	10 mL
Milk	½ cup	125 mL
Lemon pepper	½-1 tsp.	2-5 mL
Cooked medium fresh (or frozen, thawed) shrimp	½ lb.	225 g
Chow mein noodles	½ cup	125 mL

Heat first amount of cooking oil in medium frying pan. Add onion, celery and green pepper. Sauté until soft.

Cook pasta in boiling water, second amount of cooking oil and salt in large uncovered pot or Dutch oven for 5 to 7 minutes, stirring occasionally, until tender but firm. Drain. Return pasta to pot.

Stir soup, parsley, milk and lemon pepper together vigorously in large bowl. Add onion mixture and pasta.

Add shrimp. Stir together lightly. Turn into ungreased 2 quart (2 L) casserole.

Top with chow mein noodles. Cover. Bake in 350°F (175°C) oven for 30 minutes until hot. Serves 4.

1 serving: 431 Calories; 11.8 g Total Fat; 806 mg Sodium; 23 g Protein; 58 g Carbohydrate; 3 g Dietary Fiber

SPICY FISH STEWP

Stewp is part stew and part soup. Crusty bread is perfect for dunking.

Cooking oil	2 tsp.	10 mL
Medium onions, halved lengthwise and thinly sliced	2	2
Garlic cloves, minced (or ½ tsp., 2 mL, powder)	2	2
Chopped celery	1½ cups	375 mL
Medium carrots, sliced	2	2
Medium green pepper, diced	1	1
Canned diced tomatoes, with juice	14 oz.	398 mL
Reserved liquid from clams, plus water to make	1 cup	250 mL
White (or alcohol-free white) wine	¼ cup	60 mL
Parsley flakes	1 tbsp.	15 mL
Dried sweet basil	½ tsp.	2 mL
Thyme leaves	½ tsp.	2 mL
Bay leaves	2	2
Hot red chili peppers, chopped (or ½-1 tsp., 2-5 mL, dried crushed chilies)	1-2	1-2
Firm white fish fillets, cut into 1½ inch (3.8 cm) squares	½ lb.	225 g
Salt	½ tsp.	2 mL
Pepper, sprinkle		
Very small (bay) scallops	4 oz.	113 g
Canned baby clams, drained and liquid reserved	5 oz.	142 g

Heat cooking oil in large pot or Dutch oven. Add onion and garlic. Sauté until soft. Do not brown.

Add next 11 ingredients. Stir together. Cover. Simmer for 20 minutes.

Add fish pieces, salt and pepper. Stir gently. Cover. Cook for 5 minutes.

Add scallops and clams. Cover. Cook for 5 minutes until scallops are opaque. Discard bay leaves. Makes 7 cups (1.75 L), enough to serve 4.

1 serving: 214 Calories; 3.9 g Total Fat; 746 mg Sodium; 23 g Protein; 20 g Carbohydrate; 4 g Dietary Fiber

Pictured on page 143.

Delicious herbed vegetables

Garlic clove, minced	1	1
Coarsely chopped onion	1 cup	250 mL
Olive (or cooking) oil	1 tbsp.	15 mL
Medium zucchini, with peel, diced	1	1
Diced green, red, orange or yellow pepper	1 cup	250 mL
Sliced fresh mushrooms	1 cup	250 mL
Canned diced tomatoes, drained	28 oz.	796 mL
Salt	1/2 tsp.	2 mL
Dried sweet basil	1 tsp.	5 mL
Granulated sugar	1 tsp.	5 mL
Dried whole oregano	1/4 tsp.	1 mL
Ground thyme	1/4 tsp.	1 mL
Large (not jumbo) shell pasta (about 8 oz., 225 g)	3 cups	750 mL
Boiling water	2 1/2 qts.	2.5 L
Cooking oil (optional)	1 tbsp.	15 mL
Salt	2 tsp.	10 mL
Grated Parmesan cheese, sprinkle (optional)	2 tbsp.	30 mL

Sauté garlic and onion in olive oil in large non-stick frying pan for 4 minutes until onion is soft.

Add next 9 ingredients. Stir together well. Cover. Simmer for 15 minutes.

Cook pasta in boiling water, cooking oil and second amount of salt in large uncovered pot or Dutch oven for 10 to 12 minutes, stirring occasionally, until tender but firm. Drain. Return pasta to pot. Pour vegetable mixture over top. Toss together well to coat.

Sprinkle with Parmesan cheese. Serves 4 to 6.

1 serving: 359 Calories; 5.3 g Total Fat; 677 mg Sodium; 12 g Protein; 68 g Carbohydrate; 6 g Dietary Fiber

MEATLESS CHILI

This long list of ingredients looks intimidating but persevere and you will have a great spicy meal. Tender vegetables and full of beans. Serve with a hearty bread.

Cooking oil	1 tbsp.	15 mL
Garlic cloves, minced (or ½ tsp., 2 mL, powder)	2	2
Sliced celery	1½ cups	375 mL
Chopped onion	1 cup	250 mL
Sliced fresh mushrooms	2 cups	500 mL
Medium red pepper, diced	1	1
Medium green pepper, diced	1	1
Diced (½ inch, 12 mm) zucchini, with peel	3 cups	750 mL
Finely diced or grated carrot	¾ cup	175 mL
Canned stewed tomatoes, with juice, chopped	2 x 14 oz.	2 x 398 mL
Canned chopped green chilies, with liquid	4 oz.	114 mL
Canned mixed beans, drained	2 x 19 oz.	2 x 540 mL
Canned pinto (or romano) beans, drained	14 oz.	398 mL
Frozen kernel corn (or 1 can, 12 oz., 341 mL, drained)	1½ cups	375 mL
Beer (or water)	1 cup	250 mL
Canned green lentils, drained	19 oz.	540 mL
Prepared mustard	1 tbsp.	15 mL
Chili powder	1-2 tsp.	5-10 mL
Ground cumin	1 tsp.	5 mL
Salt	1 tsp.	5 mL
Dried whole oregano	½ tsp.	2 mL
Pepper	¼ tsp.	1 mL

Heat cooking oil in large pot or Dutch oven. Add garlic, celery and onion. Sauté until onion is soft.

Add mushrooms, red and green peppers, zucchini and carrot. Cook, stirring often, for 3 to 4 minutes until mushrooms and zucchini begin to soften.

(continued on next page)

Stir in remaining 13 ingredients. Bring to a slow boil. Cover. Simmer for 15 minutes to blend flavors. Remove cover. Boil slowly for 15 minutes to reduce liquid. Makes 13 cups (3.25 L), enough to serve 6.

1 serving: *379 Calories; 4.7 g Total Fat; 1418 mg Sodium; 19 g Protein; 69 g Carbohydrate; 16 g Dietary Fiber*

Pictured on page 89.

MACARONI SPECIAL

Has a crunchy topping. Good combinations.

Chopped onion	¹/₂ cup	125 mL
Hard margarine (or butter)	2 tsp.	10 mL
Condensed tomato soup	10 oz.	284 mL
Water	¹/₂ cup	125 mL
Grated medium Cheddar cheese	1 cup	250 mL
Elbow macaroni	2 cups	500 mL
Boiling water	3 qts.	3 L
Cooking oil (optional)	1 tbsp.	15 mL
Salt	2 tsp.	10 mL
TOPPING		
Hard margarine (or butter)	2 tbsp.	30 mL
Dry bread crumbs	¹/₂ cup	125 mL

Sauté onion in margarine in large frying pan until soft.

Add soup, water and cheese. Stir together until cheese is melted. Remove from heat.

Cook pasta in boiling water, cooking oil and salt in large uncovered pot or Dutch oven for 5 to 7 minutes, stirring occasionally, until tender but firm. Drain. Return pasta to pot. Add tomato soup mixture to pasta. Stir. Turn into ungreased 2 quart (2 L) casserole.

Topping: Melt margarine in small saucepan. Stir in bread crumbs. Sprinkle over all. Bake, uncovered, in 350°F (175°C) oven for 30 minutes. Makes 8 cups (2 L).

1¹/₂ cups (375 mL): *386 Calories; 15.3 g Total Fat; 684 mg Sodium; 13 g Protein; 49 g Carbohydrate; 2 g Dietary Fiber*

BEAN DISH

A bit of a pleasant nip. Good eating.

Canned beans in tomato sauce	14 oz.	398 mL
Canned chick peas (garbanzo beans), drained	19 oz.	540 mL
Canned kidney beans, drained	14 oz.	398 mL
Chopped onion	1½ cups	375 mL
Cooking oil	2 tsp.	10 mL
All-purpose flour	2 tbsp.	30 mL
Tomato sauce	7½ oz.	213 mL
Ketchup	½ cup	125 mL
Brown sugar, packed	¼ cup	60 mL
White vinegar	2 tbsp.	30 mL
Hot pepper sauce	½-¾ tsp.	2-4 mL

Combine all 3 beans in ungreased 2 quart (2 L) casserole.

Sauté onion in cooking oil in medium frying pan until soft.

Mix in flour. Stir in tomato sauce until boiling and thickened. Add ketchup, brown sugar, vinegar and hot pepper sauce. Stir together. Add to casserole. Stir lightly. Bake, uncovered, in 350°F (175°C) oven for about 45 minutes. Makes 6 cups (1.5 L).

1½ cups (375 mL): 436 Calories; 5 g Total Fat; 1469 mg Sodium; 18 g Protein; 88 g Carbohydrate; 17 g Dietary Fiber

Paré Pointer

That very noisy green animal is a frog horn.

Colorful surprises await you in this rice dish.

Long grain white rice	2 cups	500 mL
Water	4 cups	1 L
Salt	1 tsp.	5 mL
Canned chopped green chilies, drained	2 × 4 oz.	2 × 114 mL
Medium tomatoes, sliced	2	2
Salt, sprinkle		
Pepper, sprinkle		
Dried sweet basil, sprinkle		
Grated part-skim mozzarella cheese	¾ cup	175 mL
Milk	⅔ cup	150 mL
Grated medium Cheddar cheese	1 cup	250 mL

Cook rice in water and salt in covered medium saucepan for 15 to 20 minutes until tender and water is absorbed. Spoon ½ of rice into greased 3 quart (3 L) casserole.

Cover rice with green chilies. Arrange tomato slices over green chilies, overlapping if needed. Sprinkle with salt, pepper and basil. Scatter mozzarella cheese over top. Pour milk around edge.

Cover with remaining ½ of rice. Sprinkle with Cheddar cheese. Cover. Bake in 325°F (160°C) oven for about 40 minutes. Remove cover. Bake for 15 minutes. Makes 9 cups (2.25 L).

1½ cups (375 mL): 381 Calories; 9.9 g Total Fat; 669 mg Sodium; 15 g Protein; 57 g Carbohydrate; 1 g Dietary Fiber

The best coal miners are hippies. They dig.

PORK STEW WITH ROTINI

Quite colorful. Cooking pasta separately keeps it firmer.

Cooking oil	2 tsp.	10 mL
Pork roast, trimmed of fat, cut into 1 inch (2.5 cm) cubes	1 lb.	454 g
Salt	½ tsp.	2 mL
Pepper	¼ tsp.	1 mL
Garlic cloves, minced (or ½ tsp., 2 mL powder)	2	2
Sliced carrot, ½ inch (12 mm) thick	2 cups	500 mL
Canned diced tomatoes, with juice	28 oz.	796 mL
Tomato (or vegetable) juice	1 cup	250 mL
Dried whole oregano, crushed	1 tsp.	5 mL
Granulated sugar	1 tsp.	5 mL
Medium zucchini, halved lengthwise and sliced ½ inch (12 mm) thick	2	2
Rotini (spiral pasta)	3 cups	750 mL
Boiling water	3 qts.	3 L
Cooking oil (optional)	1 tbsp.	15 mL
Salt	2 tsp.	10 mL

Heat first amount of cooking oil in large non-stick frying pan. Add pork. Sauté for about 4 minutes.

Add first amount of salt, pepper, garlic and carrot. Cook for 3 to 4 minutes until carrot is bright colored and pork is browned.

Stir in next 4 ingredients. Cover. Simmer for 30 to 35 minutes, stirring occasionally, until carrot is tender-crisp.

Stir in zucchini. Cook, uncovered, for 10 to 15 minutes until zucchini is tender-crisp.

Cook pasta in boiling water, second amounts of cooking oil and salt in large uncovered pot or Dutch oven for 10 to 12 minutes, stirring occasionally, until tender but firm. Drain. Add to stew. Stir together well. Serves 4.

1 serving: 528 Calories; 10.7 g Total Fat; 993 mg Sodium; 37 g Protein; 71 g Carbohydrate; 7 g Dietary Fiber

Pictured on page 107.

You will need a large, deep frying pan for this tasty meal.

Pork chops (¹/₂ inch, 12 mm, thick), trimmed of fat	1¹/₂ lbs.	680 g
Garlic powder	¹/₈ tsp.	0.5 mL
Pepper	¹/₈ tsp.	0.5 mL
Cooking oil	1 tsp.	5 mL
Frozen hash brown potatoes (or shredded potato)	4 cups	1 L
Diced carrot	1 cup	250 mL
Sliced fresh mushrooms	1 cup	250 mL
Onion slices (¹/₄ inch, 6 mm, thick)	4-6	4-6
Condensed cream of mushroom soup	10 oz.	284 mL
Milk	¹/₂ cup	125 mL
Salt, sprinkle (optional)		
Pepper, sprinkle		

Sprinkle pork chops with garlic powder and pepper. Brown both sides well in cooking oil in large frying pan. Transfer to plate. Drain any fat from pan.

Combine potatoes, carrot and mushrooms in same frying pan. Arrange pork chops over top.

Lay 1 onion slice on each pork chop.

Stir soup, milk, salt and pepper together in small bowl. Pour over top, being sure to get some on each pork chop. Cover. Cook for 30 minutes. Move pork chops aside to stir potato mixture gently. Replace chops. Cover. Cook for about 15 minutes until vegetables are tender. Serves 4.

1 serving: 495 Calories; 18.4 g Total Fat; 743 mg Sodium; 31 g Protein; 52 g Carbohydrate; 6 g Dietary Fiber

Paré Pointer

This is a non profit store. We didn't intend it to be but we are.

PORK AND RICE DISH

Appetizing cheesy topping covers the chops.

Pork chops (¾ inch, 2 cm, thick), trimmed of fat	6	6
Cooking oil	2 tsp.	10 mL
Salt, sprinkle		
Pepper, sprinkle		
Boiling water	½ cup	125 mL
Beef bouillon powder	1 tbsp.	15 mL
Granulated sugar	1 tsp.	5 mL
Pepper	¼ tsp.	1 mL
Onion flakes	1 tbsp.	15 mL
Uncooked long grain white rice	1 cup	250 mL
Canned stewed tomatoes, with juice, broken up	2 × 14 oz.	2 × 398 mL
TOPPING		
Hard margarine (or butter)	2 tbsp.	30 mL
Dry bread crumbs	½ cup	125 mL
Grated medium Cheddar cheese	¾ cup	175 mL

Brown pork chops on both sides in cooking oil in large frying pan. Sprinkle with salt and pepper.

Pour boiling water into large bowl. Add bouillon powder, sugar, pepper and onion flakes. Stir together well.

Add rice and tomatoes with juice. Stir. Pour into ungreased 9 x 13 inch (22 x 33 cm) pan. Arrange pork chops over top. Cover with foil. Bake in 350°F (175°C) oven for 45 to 60 minutes.

Topping: Melt margarine in small saucepan. Add bread crumbs and cheese. Stir. Sprinkle over all. Cover. Return to oven for about 15 minutes until pork is very tender and rice is cooked. Serves 6.

1 serving: 456 Calories; 17.1 g Total Fat; 933 mg Sodium; 30 g Protein; 45 g Carbohydrate; 2 g Dietary Fiber

Very fresh looking with pea pods over top. Complete meal with pork, vegetables and rice.

Cooking oil	2 tsp.	10 mL
Boneless pork shoulder steak, cut into ¾ inch (2 cm) cubes	1 lb.	454 g
Salt, sprinkle		
Pepper, sprinkle		
Medium carrots, cut into strips	2	2
Medium onion, sliced	1	1
Canned whole mushrooms, drained	10 oz.	284 mL
Uncooked instant white rice	2 cups	500 mL
Chicken bouillon powder	1 tbsp.	15 mL
Boiling water	2 cups	500 mL
Soy sauce	2 tbsp.	30 mL
Frozen pea pods, thawed	10 oz.	285 g
Green onions, chopped	1-2	1-2
Medium green pepper, cut into strips	1	1

Heat cooking oil in large frying pan. Add pork. Brown all sides. Turn into ungreased 2 quart (2 L) casserole. Sprinkle with salt and pepper.

Add carrot, onion, mushrooms and rice. Stir together.

Stir bouillon powder and boiling water together in small bowl. Add soy sauce. Stir. Pour over all. Cover. Bake in 350°F (175°C) oven for about 1½ hours until pork is very tender.

Stir in pea pods, green onion and green pepper. Cover. Bake for 10 to 15 minutes. Serves 4.

1 serving: 539 Calories; 21.9 g Total Fat; 1240 mg Sodium; 27 g Protein; 58 g Carbohydrate; 6 g Dietary Fiber

Paré Pointer

The best way to catch a squirrel is to act like a nut.

QUICK FIX MEAL

Only a bit more time if you brown chops first. Good either way.

Pork chops (¾ inch, 2 cm, thick), trimmed of fat	4	4
Medium potatoes, thickly sliced	3	3
Medium parsnips, quartered	2	2
Frozen kernel corn	1 cup	250 mL
Medium onion, sliced	1	1
Canned tomatoes, with juice, cut up	14 oz.	398 mL
Envelope dry onion soup mix	1 × 1½ oz.	1 × 42 g

Layer pork chops in ungreased baking dish large enough to hold in single layer. Cover pork with potato. Add layers of parsnip, corn and onion.

Stir tomatoes with juice and dry soup mix together in small bowl. Pour over top. Cover. Bake in 350°F (175°C) oven for 1½ to 2 hours until pork is very tender. Serves 4.

1 serving: 341 Calories; 7.1 g Total Fat; 1178 mg Sodium; 27 g Protein; 44 g Carbohydrate; 6 g Dietary Fiber

Variation: For an extra touch brown pork chops in 2 tsp. (10 mL) cooking oil before layering in casserole.

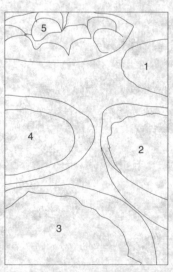

1. Spinach Onion Quiche, page 43
2. Sausage Hash, page 78
3. Chef's Salad, page 130
4. Borscht Stew, page 30
5. Beef And Dumplings, page 31

PINEAPPLE PORK AND RICE

Peachy-red color with a sweet and sour flavor.

Cornstarch	2 tbsp.	30 mL
Ground ginger	2 tsp.	10 mL
Garlic salt	1 tsp.	5 mL
Pepper	¼ tsp.	1 mL
Lean pork loin, cut into 1 inch (2.5 cm) pieces	1 lb.	454 g
Cooking oil	1 tbsp.	15 mL
Canned pineapple tidbits, with juice	14 oz.	398 mL
Brown sugar, packed	⅓ cup	75 mL
White vinegar	2 tbsp.	30 mL
Ketchup	2 tbsp.	30 mL
Soy sauce	1 tbsp.	15 mL
Canned tomato juice	10 oz.	284 mL
Water	1 cup	250 mL
Uncooked long grain white rice	1¼ cups	300 mL

Combine cornstarch, ginger, garlic salt and pepper in plastic bag. Add pork pieces, a few at a time, and shake to coat.

Heat cooking oil in large frying pan. Sauté pork until browned.

Add next 5 ingredients. Stir together. Cover. Simmer for 20 minutes.

Stir in tomato juice, water and rice. Cover. Simmer for 35 to 40 minutes, stirring after 20 minutes, until rice is cooked and pork is tender. Serves 4.

1 serving: 561 Calories; 6.9 g Total Fat; 1026 mg Sodium; 30 g Protein; 95 g Carbohydrate; 2 g Dietary Fiber

Paré Pointer

The favorite piece of clothing for an octopus on a cold day is a coat of arms.

PORK AND NOODLES

Rice noodles, vegetables and bean sprouts round out this dish. The great flavor of this stir-fry comes from the sauce.

Soy sauce	2 tbsp.	30 mL
Lemon juice	2 tsp.	10 mL
Cooking oil	2 tsp.	10 mL
Grated fresh gingerroot	1 tsp.	5 mL
Garlic cloves, minced (or ½ tsp., 2 mL, powder)	2	2
Dried crushed chilies, finely crushed	¼ tsp.	1 mL
Pork tenderloin, cut into 1 x 2 inch (2.5 x 5 cm) strips	¾ lb.	340 g
Rice stick noodles, broken up	2 cups	500 mL
Warm water	6 cups	1.5 L
Thin diagonally sliced carrot	½ cup	125 mL
Thin diagonally sliced celery	½ cup	125 mL
Coarsely chopped onion	½ cup	125 mL
Coarsely shredded cabbage	2 cups	500 mL
Fresh bean sprouts (small handful)	½ cup	125 mL
Cornstarch	1½ tbsp.	25 mL
Cold water	¾ cup	175 mL
Soy sauce	1 tbsp.	15 mL
Chili sauce (or ketchup)	1 tbsp.	15 mL
Granulated sugar	½ tsp.	2 mL

Stir first 6 ingredients together in medium bowl. Add pork strips. Press down to coat. Let stand for 15 minutes.

Place noodles in separate medium bowl. Pour warm water over top. Let stand for 15 minutes. Drain.

Turn pork and marinade into hot non-stick wok or large frying pan. Stir-fry for about 3 minutes until pork is no longer pink.

Stir in carrot, celery, onion and cabbage. Cover. Cook for about 3 minutes until vegetables are tender-crisp.

Stir in bean sprouts.

(continued on next page)

Stir cornstarch and cold water together in small cup. Add second amount of soy sauce, chili sauce and sugar. Stir together well. Add to wok. Stir until boiling and slightly thickened. Mix in rice noodles. Cover. Cook for 1 minute until heated through. Serves 4.

1 serving: 461 Calories; 5.3 g Total Fat; 913 mg Sodium; 26 g Protein; 77 g Carbohydrate; 4 g Dietary Fiber

GREEK PIZZA

Greek favorites—spinach and feta cheese.

Commercial partially baked 12 inch (30 cm) pizza crust	1	1
Bacon slices, cut into ½ inch (12 mm) pieces	8	8
Thinly sliced onion, separated into rings	2 cups	500 mL
Commercial pizza sauce	½ cup	125 mL
Frozen chopped spinach, thawed and squeezed dry	10 oz.	300 g
Grated part-skim mozzarella cheese	1 cup	250 mL
Crumbled feta cheese	½ cup	125 mL

Place crust on greased 12 inch (30 cm) pizza pan.

Cook bacon in medium frying pan until partially cooked. Drain.

Add onion rings. Sauté until onion is soft and bacon is cooked.

Spread pizza sauce over crust. Arrange spinach over top. Spread with bacon and onion. Scatter mozzarella cheese and feta cheese over top. Bake on bottom rack in 425°F (220°C) oven for 8 to 12 minutes. Cuts into 8 wedges.

1 wedge: 276 Calories; 11.6 g Total Fat; 451 mg Sodium; 12 g Protein; 31 g Carbohydrate; 3 g Dietary Fiber

Pictured on page 107.

CURRIED PORK AND MANGO SAUCE

The sauce has a nice bite to it. Delicious!

Pork tenderloin, cut into 1/2 inch (12 mm) thick medallions	1 lb.	454 g
Chili powder, sprinkle		
Cooking oil	1 tsp.	5 mL
MANGO SAUCE		
Chopped onion	1 cup	250 mL
Cooking oil	1 tsp.	5 mL
Curry paste (available in ethnic section of grocery stores)	2 tsp.	10 mL
Canned mangoes, diced, juice reserved	14 oz.	398 mL
Small red chili pepper, finely chopped (or 1/4 tsp., 1 mL, dried crushed chilies), optional	1	1
Diced zucchini, with peel	2 cups	500 mL
Diced red pepper	1 cup	250 mL
Lime juice	1 tbsp.	15 mL
Paprika	1 tsp.	5 mL
Skim evaporated milk	1/2 cup	125 mL
Coconut flavoring	1/2 tsp.	2 mL
Cornstarch	1 tbsp.	15 mL
Fresh pea pods (or frozen, thawed), about 6 oz. (170 g), sliced diagonally	2 1/2 cups	625 mL
Angel hair pasta	10 oz.	285 g
Boiling water	3 qts.	3 L
Cooking oil (optional)	1 tbsp.	15 mL
Salt	1 tbsp.	15 mL
Flake coconut, toasted	2 tsp.	10 mL

Sprinkle both sides of each pork medallion with chili powder. Sauté pork in cooking oil in large non-stick frying pan until browned on both sides. Remove to plate. Keep warm.

Mango Sauce: Sauté onion in first cooking oil and curry paste in same frying pan for about 2 minutes until onion is soft.

Stir in next 6 ingredients. Cover. Cook for 4 minutes.

(continued on next page)

Combine evaporated milk, coconut flavoring and cornstarch in small cup. Mix well. Stir into zucchini mixture until boiling and thickened. Stir in ½ cup (125 mL) reserved mango juice, if needed, to thin sauce. Add pork. Simmer, uncovered, for about 8 minutes until cooked. Add pea pods. Cook for 3 to 4 minutes until tender-crisp.

Cook pasta in boiling water, second amount of cooking oil and salt in large uncovered pot or Dutch oven for 5 to 6 minutes, stirring occasionally, until tender but firm. Drain. Serve pork and mango sauce over pasta.

Sprinkle with coconut. Serves 4.

1 serving: 581 Calories; 8.2 g Total Fat; 110 mg Sodium; 40 g Protein; 87 g Carbohydrate; 8 g Dietary Fiber

Pictured on page 89.

PORK STEW

Pork is tender and flavorful. Good meal.

Lean pork, cut into ¾ inch (2 cm) cubes	1 lb.	454 g
Cooking oil	2 tsp.	10 mL
Boiling water, to cover	¾ cup	175 mL
Salt	1 tsp.	5 mL
Pepper	¼ tsp.	1 mL
Medium potatoes, diced	2	2
Medium carrots, sliced	2	2
Medium onion, sliced	1	1
Light sour cream	1 cup	250 mL
All-purpose flour	3 tbsp.	50 mL
Liquid gravy browner, for color	½ tsp.	2 mL

Sauté pork in cooking oil in large frying pan until browned. Put into ungreased 3 quart (3 L) casserole. Add boiling water. Sprinkle with salt and pepper. Cover. Bake in 350°F (175°C) oven for 45 minutes.

Add potato, carrot and onion. Cover. Bake for 45 minutes. Drain stock into measuring cup. Add water, if needed, to make 1 cup (250 mL).

Gradually whisk sour cream into flour in medium bowl. Add gravy browner. Add stock. Stir together well. Pour over pork mixture. Bake for 20 minutes. Serves 4.

1 serving: 298 Calories; 9.6 g Total Fat; 799 mg Sodium; 28 g Protein; 24 g Carbohydrate; 2 g Dietary Fiber

SAUSAGE HASH

Spicy good. Cabbage and rice are moist. Slices of rye bread go well with this.

Chopped onion	1½ cups	375 mL
Cooking oil	2 tsp.	10 mL
Ukrainian (or ham) sausage, diced	¾ lb.	340 g
Chopped cabbage	4 cups	1 L
Condensed onion soup	10 oz.	284 mL
Tomato sauce	7½ oz.	213 mL
Water	⅔ cup	150 mL
Uncooked long grain white rice	1 cup	250 mL
Salt	½ tsp.	2 mL
Pepper	¼ tsp.	1 mL
Diced tomato	1 cup	250 mL
Chopped fresh parsley, sprinkle (optional)		

Sauté onion in cooking oil in large frying pan until soft.

Add sausage and cabbage. Cover. Cook for about 5 minutes until cabbage is soft.

Stir in next 6 ingredients. Boil slowly, stirring once or twice, for about 30 minutes until rice is tender and liquid is absorbed.

Stir in tomato. Sprinkle with parsley. Makes 8 cups (2 L).

1½ cups (375 mL): 422 Calories; 20.4 g Total Fat; 1684 mg Sodium; 15 g Protein; 46 g Carbohydrate; 3 g Dietary Fiber

Pictured on page 71.

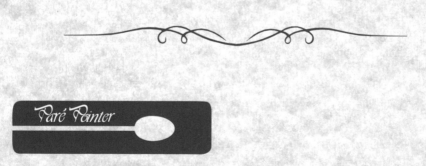

Paré Pointer

The first comment from firemen when they arrived at the burning church was "Holy Smoke."

If you prefer less spice, simply use sweet sausage rather than hot. Hot pepper sauce may also be omitted.

Spicy Italian sausage, cut into **½ inch (12 mm) slices**	1 lb.	454 g
Chopped onion	½ cup	125 mL
Chopped green pepper	½ cup	125 mL
Diced zucchini, with peel	2 cups	500 mL
Canned stewed tomatoes, with juice, **chopped**	14 oz.	398 mL
Granulated sugar	½ tsp.	2 mL
Drops of hot pepper sauce (optional)	2-4	2-4
Vermicelli	8 oz.	225 g
Boiling water	2 qts.	2 L
Cooking oil (optional)	1 tbsp.	15 mL
Salt	2 tsp.	10 mL

Cook sausage in large non-stick frying pan on both sides until browned. With slotted spoon, remove to paper towel-lined plate to drain. Drain all but 2 tsp. (10 mL) fat from pan.

Add onion, green pepper and zucchini to same frying pan. Sauté until soft.

Stir in tomatoes with juice, sugar and hot pepper sauce. Add sausage. Cover. Simmer for 15 minutes.

Cook pasta in boiling water, cooking oil and salt in large uncovered pot or Dutch oven for 6 to 7 minutes until tender but firm. Drain. Return pasta to pot. Add sausage mixture. Stir together. Makes 8 cups (2 L).

1½ cups (375 mL): 339 Calories; 12.9 g Total Fat; 579 mg Sodium; 15 g Protein; 41 g Carbohydrate; 3 g Dietary Fiber

Pictured on page 17.

ITALIAN PASTA SKILLET

Sausage, tomatoes and pasta say Italian. Use hot sausage if you like more spice.

Italian sausages, cut into ½ inch (12 mm) pieces	¾ lb.	340 g
Large onion, chopped	1	1
Garlic clove, minced (or ¼ tsp., 1 mL, powder)	1	1
Chopped fresh mushrooms	1 cup	250 mL
Medium green pepper, diced	1	1
Canned diced tomatoes, with juice	28 oz.	796 mL
Tomato (or vegetable) juice	1 cup	250 mL
Water	1 cup	250 mL
Dried sweet basil	2 tsp.	10 mL
Granulated sugar	½ tsp.	2 mL
Dried whole oregano	¼ tsp.	1 mL
Uncooked penne (about 6 oz., 170 g)	2 cups	500 mL
Grated Parmesan cheese	2 tbsp.	30 mL
Chopped fresh parsley (or 1½ tsp., 7 mL, flakes)	2 tbsp.	30 mL

Sauté sausage, onion and garlic in large frying pan until onion is soft.

Add mushrooms and green pepper. Sauté until onion and sausage are lightly browned. Drain.

Add next 7 ingredients. Stir together. Cover. Boil gently for 30 to 35 minutes until pasta is tender.

Serve with Parmesan cheese and parsley sprinkled over top. Serves 6.

1 serving: 257 Calories; 8.3 g Total Fat; 651 mg Sodium; 12 g Protein; 34 g Carbohydrate; 3 g Dietary Fiber

Paré Pointer

The first nudist convention was given very little coverage.

Pronounced ka-soo-LAY. Really good. Lots of flavor from sausage and bacon.

Sliced carrot	1½ cups	375 mL
Medium or large onion, chopped	1	1
Sliced celery	½ cup	125 mL
Water	2 cups	500 mL
Small zucchini, with peel, diced	1	1
Instant potato flakes	2 tbsp.	30 mL
Canned small white beans (or white kidney beans), drained	19 oz.	540 mL
Small link sausages	1 lb.	454 g
Bacon slices, diced	6	6
Canned stewed tomatoes, with juice, broken up	14 oz.	398 mL
Garlic powder	¼ tsp.	1 mL
TOPPING		
Hard margarine (or butter)	2 tbsp.	30 mL
Dry bread crumbs	½ cup	125 mL

Combine carrot, onion, celery and water in large frying pan. Cover. Cook until almost tender.

Add zucchini. Cook for 5 minutes. Drain. Sprinkle with potato flakes. Stir. Turn into ungreased 2 quart (2 L) casserole.

Layer beans over top.

Poke holes in sausages with tip of knife. Cook sausages and bacon in medium frying pan. Drain on paper towels. Cut sausages in half crosswise. Place sausage and bacon over beans.

Mix tomatoes with juice and garlic powder in small bowl. Pour over all.

Topping: Melt margarine in small saucepan. Stir in bread crumbs. Sprinkle over top. Bake, uncovered, in 350°F (175°C) oven for about 45 minutes. Makes 7 cups (1.75 L).

1½ cups (375 mL): 460 Calories; 26.8 g Total Fat; 1040 mg Sodium; 17 g Protein; 39 g Carbohydrate; 6 g Dietary Fiber

CHEESY WIENERS AND POTATOES

A great dish for any age.

Chopped onion	⅔ cup	150 mL
Hard margarine (or butter)	2 tsp.	10 mL
Diced potato	3 cups	750 mL
Water	⅓ cup	75 mL
Salt	½ tsp.	2 mL
Wieners, cut into ½ inch (12 mm) slices	1 lb.	454 g
All-purpose flour	3 tbsp.	50 mL
Seasoned salt	1 tsp.	5 mL
Pepper, sprinkle		
Cayenne pepper, sprinkle (optional)		
Milk	1½ cups	375 mL
Grated medium Cheddar cheese	1 cup	250 mL
Canned kernel corn, drained	12 oz.	341 mL

Sauté onion in margarine in medium saucepan until soft.

Add potato, water and salt. Cover. Cook gently for about 15 minutes, stirring occasionally, until tender and water is evaporated.

Add wieners. Stir often as wieners get plump and start to brown. This will take about 5 minutes.

Stir flour, seasoned salt, pepper and cayenne pepper together in small saucepan. Gradually whisk in milk until smooth. Add to wiener mixture. Stir until boiling and thickened.

Add cheese and corn. Stir until cheese is melted and corn is heated through. Serves 4.

1 serving: 712 Calories; 46.5 g Total Fat; 2365 mg Sodium; 28 g Protein; 47 g Carbohydrate; 4 g Dietary Fiber

Paré Pointer

Those holes in the wood are knotholes. If they're not holes, what are they?

Hard to say who likes this best—kids, moms or dads.

Chopped onion	½ cup	125 mL
Hard margarine (or butter)	1 tsp.	5 mL
Canned beans in tomato sauce	2 × 14 oz.	2 × 398 mL
Canned kidney beans, drained	14 oz.	398 mL
Wieners, cut crosswise into bite-size pieces	1 lb.	454 g
Fancy molasses	2 tbsp.	30 mL
Ketchup	¼ cup	60 mL
Brown sugar, packed	2 tbsp.	30 mL
Prepared mustard	1 tsp.	5 mL
Apple cider vinegar	1 tsp.	5 mL
Worcestershire sauce	1 tsp.	5 mL
Dry mustard	½ tsp.	2 mL

Sauté onion in margarine in small frying pan until soft. Transfer to ungreased 2 quart (2 L) casserole.

Add next 3 ingredients. Stir.

Stir remaining 7 ingredients together in small bowl. Add to casserole. Stir well. Cover. Bake in 350°F (175°C) oven for 40 to 50 minutes, stirring at half-time. Serves 6.

1 serving: 483 Calories; 23.7 g Total Fat; 1679 mg Sodium; 19 g Protein; 53 g Carbohydrate; 14 g Dietary Fiber

Variation: Use tofu wieners to make this meatless.

Paré Pointer

The first one to take a bath is the ringleader.

PINEAPPLE HAM BAKE

If you have never tried baked beans with pineapple, this is where to start. So easy. So good.

Medium red onion, chopped (see Note)	1	1
Diced or chopped cooked ham	2 cups	500 mL
Canned beans in tomato sauce	2 × 14 oz.	2 × 398 mL
Canned pineapple tidbits, drained	19 oz.	540 mL
White vinegar	1 tbsp.	15 mL
Brown sugar, packed	3 tbsp.	50 mL
Prepared mustard	1½ tsp.	7 mL

Combine red onion, ham, beans and pineapple in ungreased 2 quart (2 L) casserole.

Mix vinegar, brown sugar and mustard in small cup. Add to casserole. Stir together well. Bake, uncovered, in 350°F (175°C) oven for 30 to 40 minutes until very hot. Makes 8 cups (2 L).

1½ cups (375 mL): 291 Calories; 3.3 g Total Fat; 1383 mg Sodium; 20 g Protein; 51 g Carbohydrate; 14 g Dietary Fiber

Note: Red onions are mild. If using a stronger onion, sauté in 1 tsp. (5 mL) margarine first.

HAM AND POTATOES

A slow cooker is required for this recipe. Very tasty. Good cheese flavor. Good brunch or luncheon dish.

Frozen hash brown potatoes	1 lb.	454 g
Minced onion flakes	1 tbsp.	15 mL
Canned flakes of ham, with liquid, broken up	2 × 6½ oz.	2 × 184 g
Jar of chopped pimiento	2 oz.	57 mL
Condensed Cheddar cheese soup	10 oz.	284 mL
Milk	¾ cup	175 mL

Combine potatoes, onion flakes, ham with liquid and pimiento in 3.5 quart (3.5 L) slow cooker. Mix well.

Stir soup and milk together in small bowl. Pour over top. Cover. Cook on Low for 7 to 9 hours or on High for 3½ to 4½ hours. Makes 4⅔ cups (1.15 L).

1½ cups (375 mL): 560 Calories; 32 g Total Fat; 2423 mg Sodium; 29 g Protein; 40 g Carbohydrate; 3 g Dietary Fiber

HAM AND CABBAGE CASSEROLE

All the flavors come through in this crunchy casserole.

Skim evaporated milk	13½ oz.	385 mL
All-purpose flour	¼ cup	60 mL
Dijon mustard	2 tsp.	10 mL
Salt	½ tsp.	2 mL
Pepper	¼ tsp.	1 mL
Ground nutmeg, sprinkle		
Coarsely chopped cabbage	5 cups	1.25 L
Chopped onion	1 cup	250 mL
Hard margarine (or butter)	1 tbsp.	15 mL
Chopped cooked ham	2 cups	500 mL
Whole wheat macaroni	⅔ cup	150 mL
Boiling water	1½ qts.	1.5 L
Cooking oil (optional)	2 tsp.	10 mL
Salt	1½ tsp.	7 mL
Bread slice, processed into crumbs	1	1
Grated medium Cheddar cheese	¼ cup	60 mL

Gradually whisk evaporated milk into flour in small saucepan until smooth. Heat, stirring constantly, until sauce is boiling and thickened. Stir in mustard, first amount of salt, pepper and nutmeg. Set aside.

Sauté cabbage and onion in margarine in large non-stick frying pan for about 6 minutes until cabbage is soft. Stir sauce into cabbage mixture. Pour ½ into greased 2 quart (2 L) casserole.

Cover with ham.

Cook pasta in boiling water, cooking oil and second amount of salt in large uncovered saucepan for 6 minutes, stirring occasionally, until just tender but still slightly undercooked. Drain. Layer over ham. Cover with remaining creamed cabbage mixture.

Combine bread crumbs and cheese in small bowl. Sprinkle over surface of casserole. Bake, uncovered, in 350°F (175°C) oven for 35 minutes until bubbly and topping is browned. Makes about 5½ cups (1.4 L), enough to serve 4.

1 serving: 385 Calories; 9.9 g Total Fat; 1596 mg Sodium; 31 g Protein; 45 g Carbohydrate; 5 g Dietary Fiber

BROCCOLI HAM ROLLS

Excellent dish. Sauce has a french-fried onion flavor.

Lasagne noodles	6	6
Boiling water	2 qts.	2 L
Salt	2 tsp.	10 mL
Condensed cream of chicken soup	10 oz.	284 mL
Light sour cream	½ cup	125 mL
Milk	½ cup	125 mL
Grated medium Cheddar cheese	½ cup	125 mL
Large egg	1	1
All-purpose flour	1 tsp.	5 mL
Grated Parmesan cheese	¼ cup	60 mL
Frozen chopped broccoli, thawed and very finely chopped	2½ cups	625 mL
Onion powder	¼ tsp.	1 mL
Thin slices of cooked ham, halved lengthwise	6	6
Grated medium Cheddar cheese	½ cup	125 mL
Canned french-fried onions (add more if desired)	½ × 2¾ oz.	½ × 79 g

Cook lasagne noodles in boiling water and salt in large uncovered saucepan for 14 to 16 minutes until tender but firm. Drain. Rinse with cold water. Drain. Return pasta to saucepan.

Mix soup, sour cream, milk and first amount of Cheddar cheese in medium bowl. Pour about ⅓ to ½ into ungreased 9 x 9 inch (22 x 22 cm) pan.

Beat egg and flour together in small bowl. Stir in Parmesan cheese, broccoli and onion powder.

Lay out lasagne noodles on working surface. Place 2 pieces of ham on each noodle. Spread ⅙ of broccoli mixture over each ham slice. Roll up tightly. Cut in half crosswise. Place cut side down in pan. Pour remaining soup mixture over top.

Sprinkle with second amount of Cheddar cheese. Scatter onions over top. Cover. Bake in 350°F (175°C) oven for about 1¼ hours. Remove cover. Bake for 5 minutes. Serves 4.

1 serving: 550 Calories; 28.3 g Total Fat; 1724 mg Sodium; 32 g Protein; 43 g Carbohydrate; 4 g Dietary Fiber

A good home-cooked taste. Topping adds a great finish.

MUSHROOM CREAM SAUCE

Chopped fresh mushrooms	1 cup	250 mL
Finely chopped onion	¼ cup	60 mL
Hard margarine (or butter)	1 tsp.	5 mL
All-purpose flour	¼ cup	60 mL
Chicken bouillon powder	2 tsp.	10 mL
Paprika	½ tsp.	2 mL
Salt	1 tsp.	5 mL
Pepper	¼ tsp.	1 mL
Milk	2 cups	500 mL
Thin center ham slice (bone-in), diced	1 lb.	454 g
Medium potatoes, thinly sliced	4	4
Medium carrots, thinly sliced	4	4
Medium onion, sliced or chopped	1	1
Frozen peas, thawed	1½ cups	375 mL

TOPPING

Hard margarine (or butter)	2 tbsp.	30 mL
Dry bread crumbs	½ cup	125 mL
Grated Cheddar cheese	¼ cup	60 mL

Mushroom Cream Sauce: Sauté mushrooms and onion in margarine in medium frying pan until soft.

Stir next 5 ingredients together in medium saucepan. Gradually whisk in milk until no lumps remain. Heat and stir until boiling and thickened. Stir in mushroom mixture.

Place ham in greased 3 quart (3 L) casserole. Layer potato, carrot and onion over top. Pour sauce over all. Cover. Bake in 350°F (175°C) oven for about 1¼ hours.

Add peas. Push down so all peas are covered with sauce.

Topping: Melt margarine in small saucepan. Stir in bread crumbs and cheese. Sprinkle over casserole. Return to oven. Bake, uncovered, for 15 minutes until potato and carrot are tender. Serves 6.

1 serving: 375 Calories; 11.5 g Total Fat; 1895 mg Sodium; 26 g Protein; 43 g Carbohydrate; 5 g Dietary Fiber

LAMB STEW

Probably not Irish but delicious just the same.

Boneless leg of lamb, cut into ¾ inch (2 cm) cubes	1½ lbs.	680 g
Medium potatoes, cut into 1 inch (2.5 cm) cubes	4	4
Medium carrots, cut into bite-size pieces	4	4
Coarsely chopped onion	1 cup	250 mL
Cubed yellow turnip (rutabaga)	1½ cups	375 mL
Canned tomatoes, with juice, broken up	14 oz.	398 mL
Salt	1½ tsp.	7 mL
Pepper, generous measure	¼ tsp.	1 mL
Granulated sugar	1 tsp.	5 mL
Ground rosemary	½ tsp.	2 mL
Garlic powder (or 1 clove, minced)	¼ tsp.	1 mL
Minute tapioca	1 tbsp.	15 mL
Water	½ cup	125 mL

Combine first 5 ingredients in small roaster.

Mix remaining 8 ingredients in medium bowl. Pour over top. Cover. Bake in 300°F (150°C) oven for about 2½ to 3 hours. Makes 8 cups (2 L).

1½ cups (375 mL): 310 Calories; 7.2 g Total Fat; 994 mg Sodium; 30 g Protein; 32 g Carbohydrate; 5 g Dietary Fiber

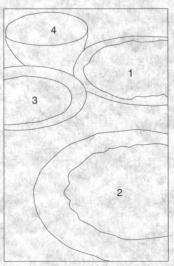

1. Taco Salad, page 135
2. Curried Pork And Mango Sauce, page 76
3. Corn Chowder, page 146
4. Meatless Chili, page 62

Surprise! This uses potatoes rather than eggplant. Great flavor.

Medium potatoes, sliced lengthwise ¹/₂ **inch (12 mm) thick**	9	9
Water, to cover		
Cooking oil	2 tsp.	10 mL
Lean ground lamb (or beef)	1¹/₂ lbs.	680 g
Chopped onion	1 cup	250 mL
Tomato sauce	2 × 7¹/₂ oz.	2 × 213 mL
Beef bouillon powder	1 tbsp.	15 mL
Granulated sugar	1 tsp.	5 mL
Parsley flakes	1 tsp.	5 mL
Ground marjoram	¹/₄ tsp.	1 mL
Garlic powder	¹/₄ tsp.	1 mL
Salt	1 tsp.	5 mL
Pepper	¹/₂ tsp.	2 mL
Grated Parmesan cheese	¹/₄ cup	60 mL
Grated part-skim mozzarella cheese	1¹/₂ cups	375 mL

Cook potato in water in large pot or Dutch oven until just tender. Potato will cook further in oven. Drain. Cool enough to handle.

Heat cooking oil in large frying pan. Add ground lamb and onion. Scramble-fry until lamb is no longer pink.

Add next 9 ingredients. Stir together. Simmer for 2 minutes. Layer in greased 9 × 13 inch (22 × 33 cm) pan as follows:

1. ¹/₂ of potato slices

2. ¹/₂ of meat sauce

3. ¹/₂ of potato slices

4. ¹/₂ of meat sauce

Sprinkle with mozzarella cheese. Bake, uncovered, in 350°F (175°C) oven for about 30 minutes until very hot. Cuts into 8 large pieces, enough to serve 8.

1 serving: 380 Calories; 17.7 g Total Fat; 1121 mg Sodium; 25 g Protein; 30 g Carbohydrate; 3 g Dietary Fiber

QUICK CHICKEN STROGANOFF

Lots of chicken in this creamy dish. Mushrooms are an added bonus.

Lean ground chicken	1 lb.	454 g
Finely chopped onion	1 cup	250 mL
Salt	1 tsp.	5 mL
Pepper	1/4 tsp.	1 mL
Garlic powder	1/4 tsp.	1 mL
Ground thyme	1/8 tsp.	0.5 mL
Sliced fresh mushrooms	2 cups	500 mL
Soy sauce	2 tbsp.	30 mL
Chicken bouillon powder	1 tbsp.	15 mL
Uncooked medium egg noodles	2 cups	500 mL
(about 4 oz., 113 g)		
Hot water	3 cups	750 mL
All-purpose flour	3 tbsp.	50 mL
Light sour cream	1 cup	250 mL
Sherry (or alcohol-free sherry)	2 tbsp.	30 mL

Spray large non-stick frying pan with no-stick cooking spray. Add first 6 ingredients. Scramble-fry for about 5 minutes.

Add mushrooms, soy sauce, bouillon powder, noodles and hot water. Make sure noodles are covered. Cover. Boil slowly for about 12 minutes until noodles are cooked.

Combine flour and sour cream in small bowl. Stir together well. Stir into chicken mixture. Stir for 2 to 3 minutes until boiling and thickened.

Stir in sherry. Makes 7 cups (1.75 L).

1 1/2 cups (375 mL): 276 Calories; 6.1 g Total Fat; 1538 mg Sodium; 29 g Protein; 24 g Carbohydrate; 2 g Dietary Fiber

Paré Pointer

The main difference between lightning and electricity is that we have to pay for electricity.

CHICKEN BROCCOLI PIE

This deep dish pie has a thick rich filling.

Lean ground chicken	1 lb.	454 g
Finely chopped onion	1/4 cup	60 mL
Finely chopped celery	1/4 cup	60 mL
All-purpose flour	2 tbsp.	30 mL
Salt	1/2 tsp.	2 mL
Pepper	1/8 tsp.	0.5 mL
Garlic powder	1/8 tsp.	0.5 mL
Milk	1 1/4 cups	300 mL
Herb-flavored non-fat spreadable cream cheese	1/2 cup	125 mL
Large egg, fork-beaten	1	1
Chopped fresh (or frozen) broccoli, cooked and drained	4 cups	1 L
Grated Edam (or Gouda or Monterey Jack) cheese	1 cup	250 mL
Pastry for 10 inch (25 cm) double crust pie		
Milk (optional)	1 tbsp.	15 mL

Scramble-fry ground chicken, onion and celery in large non-stick frying pan until onion is soft and chicken is no longer pink.

Mix in flour, salt, pepper and garlic powder. Stir in milk until boiling and thickened. Remove from heat.

Stir in cream cheese until melted.

Mix in egg, broccoli and Edam cheese.

Roll out pastry on lightly floured surface. Fit into ungreased 10 inch (25 cm) glass pie plate or 9 inch (22 cm) deep dish pie plate. Add broccoli mixture. Roll out second crust. Moisten edges of bottom crust. Put second crust in place. Trim and crimp around edge. Cut slits in top.

Brush with milk if desired. Bake on bottom rack in 350°F (175°C) oven for 45 to 50 minutes until golden. Cuts into 8 wedges.

1 wedge: 411 Calories; 21.2 g Total Fat; 676 mg Sodium; 25 g Protein; 30 g Carbohydrate; 4 g Dietary Fiber

CHICKEN VERONIQUE

The addition of grapes makes this a French pot pie.

Lean ground chicken	1 lb.	454 g
Chopped onion	2/3 cup	150 mL
Chopped celery	1/2 cup	125 mL
Cooking oil	2 tsp.	10 mL
White (or alcohol-free white) wine	1/4 cup	60 mL
Skim evaporated milk	1 cup	250 mL
All-purpose flour	1/4 cup	60 mL
Light salad dressing (or mayonnaise)	1/4 cup	60 mL
Salt	1 tsp.	5 mL
Granulated sugar	1 tsp.	5 mL
Ground cinnamon (optional)	1/16 tsp.	0.5 mL
Pepper	1/8 tsp.	0.5 mL
Halved seedless green grapes	1 cup	250 mL
LATTICE TOPPING		
Whole wheat flour	2/3 cup	150 mL
All-purpose flour	2/3 cup	150 mL
Granulated sugar	2 tsp.	10 mL
Baking powder	2 tsp.	10 mL
Salt	1/2 tsp.	2 mL
Milk	1/3 cup	75 mL
Hard margarine (or butter), melted	1/4 cup	60 mL

Scramble-fry ground chicken, onion and celery in cooking oil in large frying pan until onion is soft and chicken is no longer pink. Stir in wine. Cook for 1 minute.

Gradually whisk evaporated milk into flour in medium bowl until smooth. Add next 5 ingredients. Stir together. Stir into chicken mixture until boiling and thickened. Stir in grapes. Pour into greased 10 inch (25 cm) glass pie plate or shallow 2 quart (2 L) casserole.

Lattice Topping: Combine first 5 ingredients in medium bowl.

Add milk and margarine. Stir to form soft ball. Knead on lightly floured surface about 8 times. Roll to same size as pie plate. Cut 1/2 inch (12 mm) wide strips. Make lattice design over chicken mixture. Bake, uncovered, in 450°F (230°C) oven for about 15 minutes until bubbling and browned. Serves 4.

1 serving: 595 Calories; 21 g Total Fat; 1453 mg Sodium; 39 g Protein; 60 g Carbohydrate; 5 g Dietary Fiber

TURKEY VERONIQUE: Substitute ground turkey for ground chicken.

CHICKEN TETRAZZINI

A flavorful and pleasant meal. Parmesan cheese adds great flavor.

Cooking oil	2 tsp.	10 mL
Boneless, skinless chicken breast halves (about 4), cut into thin strips	1 lb.	454 g
Chopped onion	½ cup	125 mL
Thinly sliced fresh mushrooms	2 cups	500 mL
Salt, sprinkle		
Pepper, sprinkle		
Spaghetti	8 oz.	225 g
Boiling water	3 qts.	3 L
Cooking oil (optional)	1 tbsp.	15 mL
Salt	2 tsp.	10 mL
Condensed cream of mushroom soup	10 oz.	284 mL
Skim evaporated milk	1 cup	250 mL
Sherry (or alcohol-free sherry)	3 tbsp.	50 mL
Grated Parmesan cheese	⅓ cup	75 mL
Grated nutmeg, just a pinch		
Chicken bouillon powder	2 tsp.	10 mL
TOPPING		
Hard margarine (or butter)	1 tbsp.	15 mL
Dry bread crumbs	½ cup	125 mL
Grated Parmesan cheese	¼ cup	60 mL

Heat first amount of cooking oil in large frying pan. Add chicken, onion and mushrooms. Sauté until chicken is no longer pink. Sprinkle with salt and pepper. Transfer to ungreased 3 quart (3 L) casserole.

Cook pasta in boiling water, second amount of cooking oil and salt in large uncovered pot or Dutch oven for 11 to 13 minutes, stirring occasionally, until tender but firm. Drain. Add pasta to chicken.

Stir next 6 ingredients together in small bowl. Pour over pasta. Poke holes to allow some to reach bottom.

Topping: Melt margarine in small saucepan. Stir in bread crumbs and cheese. Sprinkle over all. Bake, uncovered, in 350°F (175°C) oven for 25 to 30 minutes until hot and golden. Serves 6.

1 serving: 445 Calories; 12.7 g Total Fat; 1014 mg Sodium; 33 g Protein; 47 g Carbohydrate; 2 g Dietary Fiber

CHICKEN FAJITA DINNER

Everyone in the family will like this one. A very child-friendly meal.

Lime juice	2 tbsp.	30 mL
Garlic cloves, minced (or ½ tsp., 2 mL, powder)	2	2
Dried crushed chilies, finely crushed	¼ tsp.	1 mL
Salt	¼ tsp.	1 mL
Pepper, sprinkle		
Boneless, skinless chicken breast halves (about 4), cut into thin strips	1 lb.	454 g
Cooking oil	2 tsp.	10 mL
Small or medium mild red or white onions, sliced and separated into rings	2	2
Medium red pepper, slivered	1	1
Medium green or yellow pepper, slivered	1	1
Frozen kernel corn, thawed	1 cup	250 mL
Medium chunky salsa	1 cup	250 mL
Water	2 tsp.	10 mL
Cornstarch	1 tsp.	5 mL
Corn chips (optional)	8½ oz.	240 g

Put first 5 ingredients into medium bowl. Stir together well. Add chicken strips. Stir. Cover. Marinate in refrigerator for 1 to 2 hours.

Heat cooking oil in large frying pan. Add chicken and marinade. Stir-fry for about 3 minutes.

Add red onion and red and green peppers. Stir together. Cover. Cook, stirring occasionally, for about 4 minutes.

Add corn and salsa. Stir. Cook, uncovered, stirring occasionally, until hot and bubbling.

Mix water and cornstarch in small cup. Stir into boiling mixture until thickened.

Sprinkle with corn chips or stir them in. They will stay crisp for about 15 minutes if stirred in. Makes 6½ cups (1.6 L).

*1½ **cups (375 mL):** 219 Calories; 3.9 g Total Fat; 1128 mg Sodium; 27 g Protein; 23 g Carbohydrate; 3 g Dietary Fiber*

Tender-crisp veggies with slivers of chicken

Cooking oil	2 tsp.	10 mL
Boneless, skinless chicken breast halves (about 4), cut into slivers	1 lb.	454 g
Garlic clove, minced (or ¼ tsp., 1 mL, powder)	1	1
Ground ginger	¼ tsp.	1 mL
Medium onion, halved lengthwise and cut into wedges	1	1
Thinly sliced carrot	½ cup	125 mL
Thinly sliced celery	1 cup	250 mL
Small broccoli florets	2 cups	500 mL
Water	1 cup	250 mL
Package Oriental dry noodle soup (original flavor), flavor packet reserved	3 oz.	85 g
Fresh bean sprouts (1 large handful)	1 cup	250 mL
Soy sauce	¼ cup	60 mL
Cornstarch	2 tsp.	10 mL
Reserved flavor packet		
Steam fried (or chow mein) noodles	½ cup	125 mL

Heat cooking oil in large frying pan. Add chicken, garlic and ginger. Stir-fry for about 3 minutes.

Add next 5 ingredients. Break up Oriental noodles and add. Cover. Cook for 2 to 3 minutes until vegetables are tender-crisp and noodles are almost cooked.

Stir in bean sprouts.

Whisk soy sauce, cornstarch and reserved flavor packet together in small bowl. Add to center of vegetable mixture. Stir until boiling and thickened.

Sprinkle with steam fried noodles. Makes 7 cups (1.75 L).

1½ cups (375 mL): 270 Calories; 8.4 g Total Fat; 1391 mg Sodium; 29 g Protein; 21 g Carbohydrate; 3 g Dietary Fiber

SWEET AND SOUR SKILLET

A favorite flavor to be sure!

Soy sauce	2 tsp.	10 mL
Garlic cloves, minced (or ½ tsp., 2 mL, powder)	2	2
Boneless, skinless chicken breast halves (about 4), cut into 1 inch (2.5 cm) pieces	1 lb.	454 g
Cooking oil	2 tsp.	10 mL
Medium onion, cut into 8 wedges	1	1
Sliced celery	1 cup	250 mL
Medium green or red pepper, cut into slivers	1	1
Coarsely shredded cabbage, packed	2 cups	500 mL
Canned tomatoes, with juice, broken up	14 oz.	398 mL
Water	¾ cup	175 mL
White vinegar	3 tbsp.	50 mL
Brown sugar, packed	2 tbsp.	30 mL
Soy sauce	1 tbsp.	15 mL
Uncooked long grain white rice	1 cup	250 mL

Stir first amount of soy sauce and garlic together in medium bowl. Add chicken. Stir well. Cover. Let stand for 15 minutes.

Heat cooking oil in large frying pan. Add chicken. Sauté until slightly browned. Remove to plate.

Put onion, celery, green pepper and cabbage into same frying pan. Cook, stirring occasionally, for 4 to 5 minutes until cabbage is soft.

Add tomatoes with juice, water, vinegar, brown sugar and second amount of soy sauce. Stir together.

Add rice and chicken. Mix. Bring to a boil. Cover. Boil slowly for 20 to 25 minutes, stirring after 15 minutes, until rice is tender. Makes 8 cups (2 L).

1½ cups (375 mL): 306 Calories; 3.4 g Total Fat; 536 mg Sodium; 24 g Protein; 44 g Carbohydrate; 3 g Dietary Fiber

Wonderful curry flavor that isn't too strong. Serve with pita bread, yogurt and perhaps a salad.

Boneless, skinless chicken breast halves (about 4), cut into 1 inch (2.5 cm) pieces	1 lb.	454 g
Diced onion	½ cup	125 mL
Curry paste (available in ethnic section of grocery stores)	1 tbsp.	15 mL
Cooking oil	1 tsp.	5 mL
Diced red pepper	½ cup	125 mL
Finely diced carrot	½ cup	125 mL
Dark raisins	¼ cup	60 mL
Condensed chicken broth	10 oz.	284 mL
Water	1 cup	250 mL
Smooth peanut butter	3 tbsp.	50 mL
Dried crushed chilies	⅛ tsp.	0.5 mL
Uncooked long grain white rice	1 cup	250 mL
Green onion, thinly sliced (optional)	1	1
Whole or coarsely chopped salted peanuts	¼ cup	60 mL

Sauté chicken, onion and curry paste in cooking oil in large non-stick frying pan until onion is soft.

Add next 8 ingredients. Stir together. Bring to a boil. Cover. Cook slowly for about 20 minutes, stirring once or twice, until rice is tender and liquid is absorbed.

Sprinkle with green onion and peanuts. Serves 4.

1 serving: 525 Calories; 15.7 g Total Fat; 695 mg Sodium; 39 g Protein; 57 g Carbohydrate; 4 g Dietary Fiber

Paré Pointer

The man who rows the boat generally doesn't have time to rock it.

CHICKEN AND BLACK BEAN STEW

Colorful and very nutritious. Has a slight bite but not overpowering.

Boneless, skinless chicken breast halves (about 4), cut into 3/4 inch (2 cm) cubes	1 lb.	454 g
Chopped onion	1½ cups	375 mL
Garlic cloves, minced (or ½ tsp., 2 mL, powder)	2	2
Cooking oil	1 tsp.	5 mL
Canned stewed tomatoes, with juice, chopped	2 × 14 oz.	2 × 398 mL
Diced carrot	1 cup	250 mL
Chopped red or orange pepper	1 cup	250 mL
Frozen kernel corn	1 cup	250 mL
Bay leaves	2	2
Ground cumin	1 tsp.	5 mL
Salt	1 tsp.	5 mL
Ground coriander	¼ tsp.	1 mL
Cayenne pepper	1/16 tsp.	0.5 mL
Canned black beans, drained	19 oz.	540 mL
Canned chopped green chilies, drained	4 oz.	114 mL
Lemon juice	1 tbsp.	15 mL

Sauté chicken, onion and garlic in cooking oil in large frying pan until onion is soft.

Add next 9 ingredients. Stir together. Bring to a boil. Boil gently, uncovered, for about 30 minutes until vegetables are soft.

Stir in beans, green chilies and lemon juice. Cover. Cook slowly for 10 minutes. Discard bay leaves. Makes 6 cups (1.5 L), enough to serve 4.

1 serving: 373 Calories; 4 g Total Fat; 1470 mg Sodium; 37 g Protein; 51 g Carbohydrate; 9 g Dietary Fiber

Pictured on page 107.

CHICKEN POT AU FEU

Poh-toh-FEUH is French for "Pot on fire." Makes an attractive full platter. A comfort food meal. If you don't have a stockpot, use a roaster on the burner.

Medium onions	2	2
Garlic cloves	3	3
Whole chicken, skin removed	3 lbs.	1.4 kg
Medium carrots, cut in half crosswise	5	5
Medium cabbage, into wedges	½	½
Medium yellow turnip (rutabaga), cut into six ½ inch (12 mm) thick slices	1	1
Celery ribs, cut into 4 inch (10 mm) lengths	2	2
Water	2 cups	500 mL
Couscous (or instant white rice), same amount as drained liquid (about 2 cups, 500 mL)		
Salt	1 tsp.	5 mL
Pepper (optional)	⅛ tsp.	0.5 mL

Place onions and garlic in cavity of chicken. Set chicken in center of stockpot.

Put next 5 ingredients around chicken. Simmer for about 1½ hours until vegetables are tender. Gently remove vegetables around chicken with slotted spoon to large platter. Transfer chicken to platter. Discard onion and cloves. Cover to keep warm. Measure remaining liquid (should be about 2 cups, 500 mL) and pour into medium saucepan.

Add same amount of couscous, salt and pepper to saucepan. Stir together. Bring to a boil. Cover. Remove from heat. Let stand for 5 minutes. Fluff with fork. Add to platter or serving bowl. Serves 6.

1 serving: 445 Calories; 4 g Total Fat; 606 mg Sodium; 35 g Protein; 66 g Carbohydrate; 7 g Dietary Fiber

ROAST CHICKEN DINNER

Chicken surrounded with vegetables.

SAUSAGE STUFFING

Sausage meat	½ lb.	225 g
Chopped onion	½ cup	125 mL
Fine dry bread crumbs	4 cups	1 L
Poultry seasoning	1½ tsp.	7 mL
Salt	¾ tsp.	4 mL
Pepper	¼ tsp.	1 mL
Parsley flakes	1 tsp.	5 mL
Water, approximately	1 cup	250 mL
Chicken bouillon powder	1 tsp.	5 mL
Roasting chicken	5 lbs.	2.3 kg
Medium potatoes, halved	4	4
Medium carrots, cut bite size	6	6
Small zucchini, with peel, cut in half crosswise	3	3
Small yellow turnip, (rutabaga), cut bite size	1	1
Hot water	1 cup	250 mL
Chicken bouillon powder	1 tsp.	5 mL

GRAVY

All-purpose flour	¼ cup	60 mL
Salt	½ tsp.	2 mL
Pepper	¼ tsp.	1 mL
Liquid gravy browner (optional)		

Sausage Stuffing: Scramble-fry sausage meat and onion in large frying pan until browned.

Add next 5 ingredients. Stir together well.

Whisk first amounts of water and bouillon powder together in small bowl. Add more or less water mixture to stuffing until damp enough to form a ball when squeezed.

Spoon stuffing into chicken. Close with skewers. Place in large roaster.

Add potato, carrot, zucchini and turnip.

(continued on next page)

Whisk second amounts of water and bouillon powder together in small bowl. Add to roaster. Cover. Bake in 325°F (160°C) oven for 1½ to 2 hours until chicken is cooked. Thermometer should read 190°F (90°C). Remove cover last few minutes to brown if desired. Strain juice into measuring cup. Skim off any fat. Add water, if needed, to make 2 cups (500 mL). Pour into small bowl.

Gravy: Whisk flour, salt, pepper and gravy browner into reserved juice. Pour into small saucepan. Heat and stir until boiling and thickened. Makes 2 cups (500 mL). Serves 6.

1 serving: 1199 Calories; 55.2 g Total Fat; 1851 mg Sodium; 83 g Protein; 89 g Carbohydrate; 6 g Dietary Fiber

SIMPLE CHICKEN BAKE

A cacciatore-type dish.

Chicken parts, skin removed	3 lbs.	1.4 kg
Cooking oil	1 tsp.	5 mL
Chopped onion	1 cup	250 mL
Penne pasta	8 oz.	225 g
Boiling water	3 qts.	3 L
Cooking oil (optional)	1 tbsp.	15 mL
Salt	2 tsp.	10 mL
Spaghetti sauce	2 cups	500 mL
Canned sliced mushrooms, drained	10 oz.	284 mL
Dried whole oregano	½ tsp.	2 mL
Salt	½ tsp.	2 mL
Pepper	¼ tsp.	1 mL

Cook chicken on both sides in cooking oil in large non-stick frying pan until no longer pink inside. Turn into ungreased 3 quart (3 L) casserole or small roaster.

Add onion to same frying pan. Sauté until soft. Add to chicken.

Cook pasta in boiling water, cooking oil and first amount of salt in large uncovered pot or Dutch oven for 8 to 10 minutes until tender but firm. Drain. Return pasta to pot.

Add remaining 5 ingredients. Stir together well. Pour over chicken. Cover. Bake in 350°F (175°C) oven for about 30 minutes until hot. Serves 4.

1 serving: 591 Calories; 13.4 g Total Fat; 1374 mg Sodium; 47 g Protein; 70 g Carbohydrate; 6 g Dietary Fiber

JAMBALAYA

Very flavorful. A mild spicy taste.

Cooking oil	2 tsp.	10 mL
Skinless chicken thighs	1½ lbs.	680 g
Salt, sprinkle		
Pepper, sprinkle		
Chopped onion	1 cup	250 mL
Garlic cloves, minced (or ½ tsp., 2 mL, powder)	2	2
Medium green pepper, chopped	1	1
Uncooked long grain white rice	1½ cups	375 mL
Diced cooked ham (½ lb., 225 g)	1¼ cups	300 mL
Canned stewed tomatoes, with juice, broken up	14 oz.	398 mL
Water	1½ cups	375 mL
White (or alcohol-free white) wine	¼ cup	60 mL
Chicken bouillon powder	2 tsp.	10 mL
Salt	1 tsp.	5 mL
Ground coriander	½ tsp.	2 mL
Cayenne pepper	⅛ tsp.	0.5 mL
Pepper	1/16 tsp.	0.5 mL
Bay leaf	1	1
Fresh medium shrimp, peeled and deveined	12	12

Heat cooking oil in large non-stick frying pan. Add chicken. Sprinkle with salt and pepper. Sauté for about 5 minutes. Remove to plate.

Combine onion, garlic and green pepper in same frying pan. Sauté until onion is soft.

Add next 11 ingredients. Stir together well. Add chicken. Cover. Simmer for 20 to 25 minutes until rice is tender. Discard bay leaf.

Add shrimp. Stir. Cook for about 5 minutes until shrimp curl and turn pink. Makes 8 cups (2 L).

1½ cups (375 mL): 411 Calories; 7.4 g Total Fat; 1501 mg Sodium; 30 g Protein; 52 g Carbohydrate; 2 g Dietary Fiber

Balsamic vinegar gives the wonderful flavor.

Cooking oil	1 tsp.	5 mL
Chicken parts, skin removed	3 lbs.	1.4 kg
Salt, sprinkle		
Pepper, sprinkle		
Large onion, chopped	1	1
Garlic clove, minced (or ¼ tsp., 1 mL, powder)	1	1
Medium carrots, sliced into ¼ inch (6 mm) coins	4	4
Medium red potatoes, cut into eighths	4	4
Water	½ cup	125 mL
Parsley flakes	1 tbsp.	15 mL
Dried sweet basil	1 tsp.	5 mL
Chicken bouillon powder	½ tsp.	2 mL
Ground thyme	1/16 tsp.	0.5 mL
Small green or red pepper, diced	1	1
Green onions, sliced	2	2
Balsamic vinegar	¼ cup	60 mL

Heat cooking oil in large non-stick frying pan. Add chicken. Brown both sides well. Sprinkle with salt and pepper. Transfer chicken to plate.

Add onion and garlic to same frying pan. Sauté until soft.

Add next 7 ingredients. Stir. Add chicken. Cover. Simmer for 25 minutes, stirring once or twice. Add more water if needed.

Add green pepper and green onion. Cover. Cook for 5 to 10 minutes until chicken and vegetables are tender.

Add vinegar. Stir. Heat through. Serves 4.

1 serving: 358 Calories; 6.4 g Total Fat; 252 mg Sodium; 40 g Protein; 35 g Carbohydrate; 5 g Dietary Fiber

Pictured on front cover.

ARROZ CON POLLO

Pronounced ah-ROHS con POH-yoh and literally means "rice with chicken." A Spanish and Mexican dish.

Chicken parts, skin removed	3¹/₂ lbs.	1.6 kg
Uncooked long grain white rice	1¹/₂ cups	375 mL
Finely chopped onion	¹/₂ cup	125 mL
Frozen peas, thawed	2 cups	500 mL
Chicken bouillon powder	1 tbsp.	15 mL
Salt	1 tsp.	5 mL
Pepper	¹/₄ tsp.	1 mL
Saffron (or turmeric)	¹/₄ tsp.	1 mL
Jar of chopped pimiento, drained	2 oz.	57 mL
Boiling water	3 cups	750 mL
Canned tomatoes, with juice, broken up	14 oz.	398 mL
Dried sweet basil	¹/₂ tsp.	2 mL
Garlic powder	¹/₄ tsp.	1 mL

Arrange chicken in greased 9 × 13 inch (22 × 33 cm) pan. Bake, uncovered, in 350°F (175°C) oven for 30 minutes. Transfer chicken to plate.

Stir remaining 12 ingredients together in same pan. Place chicken over rice mixture. Cover. Return to oven. Bake for 35 to 45 minutes until rice and chicken are tender. Serves 6.

1 serving: 395 Calories; 4.7 g Total Fat; 1050 mg Sodium; 35 g Protein; 51 g Carbohydrate; 4 g Dietary Fiber

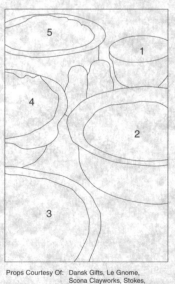

1. Tuna Penne Salad, page 123
2. Chicken And Black Bean Stew, page 100
3. Greek Pizza, page 75
4. Whiskey Stew, page 115
5. Pork Stew With Rotini, page 66

Props Courtesy Of: Dansk Gifts, Le Gnome, Scona Clayworks, Stokes, The Bay

BAKED PAELLA CASSEROLE

Pronounced pi-AY yuh. A popular mixture of shrimp, chicken and of course, rice.

Chicken parts, skin removed	3 lbs.	1.4 kg
Cooking oil	1 tbsp.	15 mL
Chopped onion	1 cup	250 mL
Chopped fresh mushrooms	1 cup	250 mL
Medium red or yellow pepper, chopped	1	1
Condensed chicken broth	10 oz.	284 mL
Water	1 cup	250 mL
Uncooked long grain white rice	1⅓ cups	325 mL
Frozen peas, thawed	1 cup	250 mL
Cooked fresh (or frozen, thawed) shrimp	4 oz.	113 g
Paprika, sprinkle		

Brown both sides of chicken in cooking oil in large frying pan. Transfer to greased 3 quart (3 L) casserole.

Add onion, mushrooms and red pepper to same frying pan. Sauté until soft.

Add chicken broth, water and rice. Bring to a boil.

Add peas and shrimp. Stir together. Pour over chicken. Cover. Bake in 350°F (175°C) oven for 30 minutes. Stir.

Sprinkle with paprika. Cover. Bake for 30 minutes until chicken and rice are tender. Serves 4.

1 serving: 567 Calories; 10 g Total Fat; 717 mg Sodium; 53 g Protein; 62 g Carbohydrate; 4 g Dietary Fiber

Paré Pointer

Mother flea was very upset. Her children had gone to the dogs.

CHICKEN AND DUMPLINGS

Old-fashioned to be sure. Just as yummy today as then.

Chicken parts, skin removed	3½ lbs.	1.6 kg
Water	7 cups	1.75 L
Chopped celery leaves and white center ribs	1 cup	250 mL
Medium onion, quartered	1	1
Bay leaf	1	1
Salt	2 tsp.	10 mL
Whole peppercorns	1 tsp.	5 mL
Diced celery	1½ cups	375 mL
Chopped onion	1½ cups	375 mL
Cooking oil	2 tsp.	10 mL
Diced carrot	1½ cups	375 mL
Chopped fresh parsley (or 2 tsp., 10 mL, flakes)	2 tbsp.	30 mL
Frozen peas	1½ cups	375 mL
Skim evaporated milk	1 cup	250 mL
All-purpose flour	¼ cup	60 mL
DUMPLINGS		
All-purpose flour	2 cups	500 mL
Baking powder	4 tsp.	20 mL
Granulated sugar	2 tsp.	10 mL
Salt	1 tsp.	5 mL
Chopped fresh parsley (or 4 tsp., 20 mL, flakes)	¼ cup	60 mL
Hard margarine (or butter)	6 tbsp.	100 mL
Milk	¾ cup	175 mL

Combine first 7 ingredients in large pot or Dutch oven. Cover. Cook for about 1½ hours. Remove chicken with slotted spoon or tongs to medium bowl. Strain broth. Skim off fat. Reserve 4 cups (1 L) broth. Remainder may be frozen for another use. Remove bones from chicken. Coarsely chop chicken.

Sauté second amounts of celery and onion in cooking oil in same pot until soft. Add carrot, parsley and reserved chicken stock. Simmer for 15 minutes until carrot is tender.

Stir in peas and chicken.

Gradually whisk evaporated milk into flour in small bowl. Stir into simmering mixture until boiling and thickened.

(continued on next page)

Dumplings: Measure first 6 ingredients into medium bowl. Cut in margarine until crumbly.

Stir in milk until moistened. Drop 12 to 14 large spoonfuls of dough over bubbling stew. Cover. Simmer for about 20 minutes until dumplings have risen. Wooden pick inserted in center of dumplings should come out clean. Serves 6.

1 serving: 681 Calories; 24.6 g Total Fat; 1781 mg Sodium; 51 g Protein; 61 g Carbohydrate; 6 g Dietary Fiber

RICE AND BROCCOLI CHICKEN

An attractive combination.

Cooking oil	1 tbsp.	15 mL
Chicken parts, skin removed	3 lbs.	1.4 kg
Garlic salt	½ tsp.	2 mL
Paprika	½ tsp.	2 mL
Pepper, sprinkle		
Medium onion, sliced	1	1
Condensed cream of mushroom soup	10 oz.	284 mL
Water	1⅔ cups	400 mL
White (or alcohol-free white) wine	⅓ cup	75 mL
Uncooked long grain white rice	1 cup	250 mL
Frozen cut broccoli, thawed	1 lb.	500 g

Heat cooking oil in large frying pan. Add chicken. Sprinkle with garlic salt, paprika and pepper. Brown both sides. Remove to medium bowl.

Add onion to same frying pan. Sauté until soft.

Stir soup vigorously in small bowl. Gradually whisk in water and wine until smooth. Add to onion. Stir together. Bring to a boil.

Add rice. Stir together well. Arrange chicken over top. Cover. Cook slowly for 15 minutes.

Add broccoli around and on top of chicken. Cover. Cook slowly for 20 to 25 minutes, stirring occasionally, to loosen any stuck rice, until chicken is cooked. Serves 4.

1 serving: 543 Calories; 14.8 g Total Fat; 948 mg Sodium; 45 g Protein; 54 g Carbohydrate; 5 g Dietary Fiber

Pictured on page 53.

VEGETABLE CHICKEN

Old-fashioned creamy chicken.

Hard margarine (or butter)	1 tbsp.	15 mL
Chicken parts, skin removed	3 lbs.	1.4 kg
Garlic salt	½ tsp.	2 mL
Pepper, sprinkle		
Water	½ cup	125 mL
White (or alcohol-free white) wine	¼ cup	60 mL
Chicken bouillon powder	1 tsp.	5 mL
Medium potatoes, cut bite size	3	3
Parsley flakes	1 tbsp.	15 mL
Salt	½ tsp.	2 mL
Ground thyme	1/16 tsp.	0.5 mL
Ground rosemary	1/16 tsp.	0.5 mL
Frozen peas, thawed	10 oz.	284 mL
Green onions, sliced	3	3
All-purpose flour	2 tbsp.	30 mL
Light sour cream	1 cup	250 mL
Granulated sugar	1 tsp.	5 mL

Melt margarine in large frying pan. Add chicken. Brown both sides. Sprinkle with garlic salt and pepper. Turn into large pot or Dutch oven.

Stir next 8 ingredients together in small bowl. Add to chicken. Cover. Simmer for about 25 minutes until potato is tender.

Add peas and green onion. Stir. Cover. Cook for 2 to 3 minutes until peas are cooked. Using slotted spoon, remove vegetables and chicken to serving platter. Cover to keep warm.

Whisk flour and sour cream together in small bowl until smooth. Add to pot. Heat and stir until just boiling and thickened. Drizzle over chicken and vegetables. Serves 4.

1 serving: 414 Calories; 12.4 g Total Fat; 923 mg Sodium; 43 g Protein; 29 g Carbohydrate; 4 g Dietary Fiber

CHICKEN AND JIFFY DUMPLINGS

The easiest dumplings going.

Cooking oil	1 tbsp.	15 mL
Boneless, skinless chicken breast halves (about 6), cut bite size	1½ lbs.	680 g
Seasoned salt	1½ tsp.	7 mL
Pepper	⅛-¼ tsp.	0.5-1 mL
Chopped onion	1¼ cups	300 mL
Chopped celery	1¼ cups	300 mL
Diced carrot	2½ cups	625 mL
Condensed chicken broth	10 oz.	284 mL
Water	1¾ cups	425 mL
Chicken bouillon powder	4 tsp.	20 mL
Parsley flakes	1 tbsp.	15 mL
Ground thyme	⅛ tsp.	0.5 mL
Evaporated milk (small can)	⅔ cup	150 mL
All-purpose flour	¼ cup	60 mL
Refrigerator country-style biscuits (10 per tube)	12 oz.	340 g

Heat cooking oil in large frying pan. Add chicken. Sprinkle with seasoned salt and pepper. Stir-fry to brown quickly. Remove to medium bowl.

Add next 8 ingredients to same frying pan. Stir together. Cover. Cook slowly until vegetables are tender.

Gradually whisk milk into flour in small bowl until no lumps remain. Stir into vegetables until boiling and thickened. Add chicken. Stir.

Cut each biscuit into 2 layers. Arrange over top. Cover. Simmer slowly for about 20 minutes until biscuits are cooked. They will be puffy and white. Serves 6.

1 serving: 407 Calories; 8.5 g Total Fat; 1730 mg Sodium; 37 g Protein; 44 g Carbohydrate; 3 g Dietary Fiber

BRUNSWICK STEW

A tasty hearty stew. A good chance to try okra if you never have.

Bacon slices, diced	2	2
Chicken thighs (about 12), skin removed	3½ lbs.	1.6 kg
Garlic salt, sprinkle		
Pepper, sprinkle		
Large onion, coarsely chopped	1	1
Condensed chicken broth	10 oz.	284 mL
Water	1 cup	250 mL
Canned diced tomatoes, with juice	14 oz.	398 mL
Granulated sugar	2 tsp.	10 mL
Dried rosemary, crushed	½ tsp.	2 mL
Thyme leaves	½ tsp.	2 mL
Bay leaf	1	1
Medium potatoes, cut into 1½ inch (3.8 cm) chunks	3	3
Frozen lima beans	2 cups	500 mL
Frozen baby okra, each cut into 2-3 pieces	8 oz.	250 g
Frozen kernel corn	2 cups	500 mL
Medium red pepper, diced	1	1
Worcestershire sauce	2 tsp.	10 mL
Salt	½ tsp.	2 mL

Cook bacon in large frying pan. Remove with slotted spoon to paper towel to drain.

Brown both sides of chicken in bacon fat in same frying pan. Sprinkle with garlic salt and pepper. Transfer to large pot or Dutch oven.

Sauté onion in same frying pan until soft. Add to pot.

Add next 7 ingredients. Stir together. Cover. Simmer for 30 minutes, stirring occasionally.

Add remaining 7 ingredients. Add bacon. Stir. Simmer, uncovered, for 30 to 40 minutes until potato is tender and stew is thickened. Discard bay leaf. Makes 8 cups (2 L) vegetables and 12 pieces of chicken, enough to serve 6.

1 serving: 423 Calories; 11.3 g Total Fat; 885 mg Sodium; 38 g Protein; 44 g Carbohydrate; 7 g Dietary Fiber

Tender chicken with a slight hint of caramel. Wonderful aroma.

All-purpose flour	¼ cup	60 mL
Garlic salt (or salt)	1 tsp.	5 mL
Pepper	⅛ tsp.	0.5 mL
Cayenne pepper, sprinkle		
Chicken parts, skin removed	8	8
Cooking oil	1 tbsp.	15 mL
Cooking oil	1 tsp.	5 mL
Chopped onion	1 cup	250 mL
Chopped celery	1 cup	250 mL
Rye whiskey	3 tbsp.	50 mL
Brown sugar, packed	1 tbsp.	15 mL
Condensed chicken broth	10 oz.	284 mL
Water	1 cup	250 mL
Diced carrot	1½ cups	375 mL
Fresh (or frozen) green beans, cut or frenched	1½ cups	375 mL
Whole new baby potatoes, with skin (or large red potatoes, cut into chunks)	1½ lbs.	680 g
Water	1 tbsp.	15 mL
Cornstarch	1 tbsp.	15 mL

Stir first 4 ingredients together in pie plate or shallow dish.

Dip chicken into flour mixture to coat. Brown both sides in first amount of cooking oil in large frying pan. Transfer to large pot or Dutch oven.

Add second amount of cooking oil to same frying pan. Add onion and celery. Sauté until golden. Add to chicken.

Add next 7 ingredients to pot. Stir together. Cover. Simmer for about 30 minutes until potato and carrot are tender. Drain liquid into small saucepan.

Mix second amount of water and cornstarch in small cup. Stir into liquid. Heat and stir until boiling and thickened. Pour over stew. Serves 4.

1 serving: 541 Calories; 9.6 g Total Fat; 980 mg Sodium; 40 g Protein; 68 g Carbohydrate; 7 g Dietary Fiber

Pictured on page 107.

CHICKEN STRATA

This can be made ahead and refrigerated overnight or can be made at least three hours ahead.

Ground chicken	1½ lbs.	680 g
Finely chopped onion	½ cup	125 mL
Finely chopped green pepper	¼ cup	60 mL
Cooking oil	2 tsp.	10 mL
Salt, sprinkle		
Pepper, sprinkle		
Bread slices, crusts removed	6-8	6-8
Frozen peas, thawed	10 oz.	284 mL
Non-fat process Cheddar cheese slices	6	6
Bread slices, crusts removed	6	6
Large eggs	5	5
Condensed cream of mushroom soup	10 oz.	284 mL
Milk	1¾ cups	425 mL
Poultry seasoning	¼ tsp.	1 mL

Scramble-fry ground chicken, onion and green pepper in cooking oil in large frying pan until no longer pink. Drain. Sprinkle with salt and pepper.

Cover bottom of greased 9 x 13 inch (22 x 33 cm) pan with first amount of bread slices, cutting to fit. Spoon chicken mixture over bread. Scatter peas over top. Lay cheese slices over peas. Cover with second amount of bread slices.

Beat eggs in medium bowl until smooth. Add remaining 3 ingredients. Mix. Pour over all. Cover and chill for 3 hours or overnight. Bake, uncovered, in 350°F (175°C) oven for about 1 hour until knife inserted in center comes out clean. Serves 6.

1 serving: 495 Calories; 13.9 g Total Fat; 1161 mg Sodium; 47 g Protein; 44 g Carbohydrate; 3 g Dietary Fiber

TURKEY STRATA: Use ground turkey instead of ground chicken.

Vegetables in a stuffing crust. Excellent.

Hard margarine (or butter)	2 tbsp.	30 mL
Finely chopped onion	²/₃ cup	150 mL
Finely chopped celery	²/₃ cup	150 mL
Fine dry bread crumbs	2 cups	500 mL
Parsley flakes	1 tbsp.	15 mL
Ground sage	¼-½ tsp.	1-2 mL
Pepper	¼ tsp.	1 mL
Hot water	¼ cup	60 mL
Milk	¼ cup	60 mL
Condensed chicken broth	10 oz.	284 mL
All-purpose flour	⅓ cup	75 mL
Frozen mixed vegetables	2 cups	500 mL
Celery salt	¼ tsp.	1 mL
Onion powder	⅛ tsp.	0.5 mL
Pepper, sprinkle		
Diced cooked turkey (or chicken)	2 cups	500 mL

Melt margarine in large frying pan. Add onion and celery. Sauté until very soft. Remove from heat.

Stir in next 4 ingredients. Gradually mix in hot water and milk. You should be able to squeeze some in your hand and it will hold its shape. Reserve ½ cup (125 mL) crumb mixture. Press remaining crumb mixture in bottom and up sides of greased 9 inch (22 cm) pie plate.

Gradually whisk chicken broth into flour in small saucepan until smooth. Heat and stir until boiling and thickened.

Add remaining 5 ingredients. Stir. Pour into stuffing crust. Sprinkle with reserved crumb mixture. Bake, uncovered, in 350°F (175°C) oven for 30 minutes until heated through. Let stand for 10 minutes. Cuts into 6 wedges.

1 wedge: 351 Calories; 7.2 g Total Fat; 777 mg Sodium; 26 g Protein; 46 g Carbohydrate; 1 g Dietary Fiber

TURKEY WITH CRANBERRY RICE

Nice combination of flavors.

Cooking oil	2 tsp.	10 mL
Thin turkey cutlets, cut into thin strips	1 lb.	454 g
Diced onion	1 cup	250 mL
Thinly sliced celery	1 cup	250 mL
Water	1½ cups	375 mL
Grated peel and juice of 1 large orange	¾ cup	175 mL
Jalapeño pepper jelly	½ cup	125 mL
Garlic salt	½ tsp.	2 mL
Pepper, sprinkle		
Package long grain and wild rice mix, with seasoning packet	6½ oz.	180 g
Fresh (or frozen) cranberries	1 cup	250 mL
Chopped toasted almonds (or pecans)	2 tbsp.	30 mL
Chopped fresh parsley	2 tbsp.	30 mL

Heat cooking oil in large frying pan. Add turkey strips, onion and celery. Sauté until onion is soft.

Add next 6 ingredients. Stir together. Cover. Simmer for 30 minutes.

Stir in cranberries. Cover. Cook for 5 to 10 minutes until rice is tender. Stir.

Sprinkle with almonds and parsley just before serving. Makes 6 cups (1.5 L).

1½ cups (375 mL): 487 Calories; 7.7 g Total Fat; 1255 mg Sodium; 32 g Protein; 76 g Carbohydrate; 6 g Dietary Fiber

The ocean should be clean—it uses tide morning and night.

Good texture and flavor. Mushrooms are tasty.

Cooking oil	1 tsp.	5 mL
Ground turkey	1 lb.	454 g
Finely chopped onion	½ cup	125 mL
Sliced fresh mushrooms	1 cup	250 mL
Salt	½ tsp.	2 mL
Pepper	¼ tsp.	1 mL
Condensed cream of chicken soup	10 oz.	284 mL
Condensed beef broth	10 oz.	284 mL
Light sour cream	1 cup	250 mL
Lemon juice	1 tsp.	5 mL
Uncooked broad egg noodles (about 4 cups, 1 L)	8 oz.	225 g
Frozen peas (or green beans)	2 cups	500 mL

Heat cooking oil in large frying pan. Add ground turkey, onion and mushrooms. Scramble-fry until lightly browned. Sprinkle with salt and pepper.

Add soup, beef broth, sour cream and lemon juice. Heat and stir until very hot.

Place noodles and peas in bottom of ungreased 3 quart (3 L) casserole. Gently pour turkey mixture over top. Do not stir. Cover. Bake in 350°F (175°C) oven for 40 to 45 minutes until noodles are tender but firm. Makes 7 cups (1.75 L).

*1½ **cups (375 mL):** 476 Calories; 12.6 g Total Fat; 1366 mg Sodium; 37 g Protein; 53 g Carbohydrate; 5 g Dietary Fiber*

CHICKEN STROGANOFF: Substitute ground chicken for ground turkey.

BEEF STROGANOFF: Substitute ground beef for ground turkey.

Paré Pointer

The only way he ever says a mouthful is to talk while he's eating.

CRAB SALAD

Delicious luncheon salad. Prepare ahead and assemble at the last minute.

Cooked fresh (or frozen or imitation) crabmeat, cartilage removed, broken up	2 cups	500 mL
Large hard-boiled eggs, chopped	3	3
Thinly sliced celery	½ cup	125 mL
Chopped pimiento	1 tbsp.	15 mL
Salt, sprinkle		
Pepper, sprinkle		
Chopped lettuce	6 cups	1.5 L
DRESSING		
Light salad dressing (or mayonnaise)	¾ cup	175 mL
Milk	3 tbsp.	50 mL
Granulated sugar	½ tsp.	2 mL
Seasoned salt	½ tsp.	2 mL
Paprika	½ tsp.	2 mL

Combine first 6 ingredients in medium bowl.

Put lettuce into large bowl.

Dressing: Stir salad dressing, milk, sugar, seasoned salt and paprika together in small bowl. Reserve ⅓ of dressing. Pour ⅔ of dressing over lettuce just before serving. Toss together. Divide among 4 plates. Divide crabmeat mixture over lettuce. Drizzle with remaining ⅓ of dressing. Serves 4.

1 serving: 282 Calories; 17.1 g Total Fat; 1370 mg Sodium; 20 g Protein; 11 g Carbohydrate; 1 g Dietary Fiber

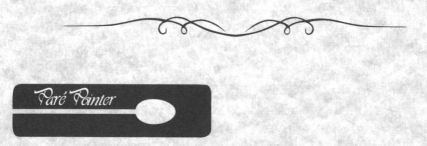

There is no harm in taking a stand providing you are facing the right way.

Also contains tuna and shrimp. A new spin on coleslaw.

Small shell pasta	1½ cups	375 mL
Boiling water	2 qts.	2 L
Cooking oil (optional)	2 tsp.	10 mL
Salt	1½ tsp.	7 mL
Grated cabbage, lightly packed	3 cups	750 mL
Grated carrot	½ cup	125 mL
Thinly sliced celery	½ cup	125 mL
Chopped green onion	½ cup	125 mL
Canned solid white tuna, drained and broken up	6½ oz.	184 g

DRESSING

Light salad dressing (or mayonnaise)	½ cup	125 mL
Milk	2 tbsp.	30 mL
White vinegar	1 tsp.	5 mL
Granulated sugar	½ tsp.	2 mL
Onion powder	¼ tsp.	1 mL
Celery salt	⅛ tsp.	0.5 mL
Cooked small fresh (or frozen, thawed) shrimp	¼ lb.	113 g

Cook pasta in boiling water, cooking oil and salt in large uncovered pot or Dutch oven for 8 to 11 minutes, stirring occasionally, until tender but firm. Drain. Rinse with cold water. Drain well. Return pasta to pot.

Add cabbage, carrot, celery, green onion and tuna. Toss together.

Dressing: Measure all 6 ingredients into small bowl. Stir together. Pour over pasta mixture. Toss to coat. Divide among 6 plates or serve in large bowl.

Sprinkle shrimp over top. Serves 6.

1 serving: 223 Calories; 6.6 g Total Fat; 348 mg Sodium; 14 g Protein; 26 g Carbohydrate; 2 g Dietary Fiber

PASTA HAM SALAD

Sweet with a slight tang. The ham adds flavor as well.

Elbow macaroni	2 cups	500 mL
Boiling water	3 qts.	3 L
Cooking oil (optional)	1 tbsp.	15 mL
Salt	2 tsp.	10 mL
Diced cooked ham	2 cups	500 mL
Thinly sliced celery	¾ cup	175 mL
Grated carrot	⅓ cup	75 mL
Chopped green onion	⅓ cup	75 mL
DRESSING		
Light salad dressing (or mayonnaise)	1 cup	250 mL
White vinegar	1 tbsp.	15 mL
Granulated sugar	1 tbsp.	15 mL
Sweet pickle relish	¼ cup	60 mL
Shredded lettuce	6 cups	1.5 L

Cook pasta in boiling water, cooking oil and salt in large uncovered pot or Dutch oven for 5 to 7 minutes, stirring occasionally, until tender but firm. Drain. Rinse with cold water. Drain. Turn into large bowl.

Add ham, celery, carrot and green onion. Stir together.

Dressing: Stir all 4 ingredients together in small bowl. Pour over salad. Toss to coat.

Scatter lettuce on 6 plates or on 1 large platter. Divide salad over top. Serves 6.

1 serving: 350 Calories; 13.5 g Total Fat; 1030 mg Sodium; 16 g Protein; 41 g Carbohydrate; 2 g Dietary Fiber

Paré Pointer

The only way he will keep a check on his waist would be to wear a gingham jacket.

Pronounced PEH-nay. Salad and dressing complement each other.
Leftovers keep well in the refrigerator for lunch the next day.

DRESSING

Cooking oil	1/4 cup	60 mL
White vinegar	1/3 cup	75 mL
Granulated sugar	3 tbsp.	50 mL
Dried sweet basil	1 1/2 tsp.	7 mL
Dried whole oregano	1/2 tsp.	2 mL
Garlic powder	1/4 tsp.	1 mL
Salt	1/2 tsp.	2 mL
Pepper	1/4 tsp.	1 mL
Penne pasta	3 1/2 cups	875 mL
Boiling water	3 qts.	3 L
Cooking oil (optional)	1 tbsp.	15 mL
Salt	1 tbsp.	15 mL
Frozen peas	2 cups	500 mL
Water	1/2 cup	125 mL
Canned solid white tuna, drained and broken up	2 x 6 1/2 oz.	2 x 184 g
Grated cabbage, lightly packed	2 cups	500 mL
Medium tomatoes, diced	2	2
Frozen kernel corn, thawed	1/2 cup	125 mL
Grated Parmesan cheese (optional)	2 tbsp.	30 mL
Chopped green onion	1/4 cup	60 mL

Dressing: Measure first 8 ingredients into small bowl. Stir together well. Let stand for about 30 minutes to blend flavors. Makes 3/4 cup (175 mL).

Cook pasta in boiling water, cooking oil and salt in large uncovered pot or Dutch oven for 10 to 12 minutes, stirring occasionally, until tender but firm. Drain. Rinse with cold water. Drain well. Turn into large bowl.

Cook peas in second amount of water in small saucepan for about 3 minutes. Drain. Rinse with cold water. Drain well. Add to pasta.

Add tuna, cabbage, tomato, corn, Parmesan cheese and green onion. Stir lightly. Add dressing. Toss together. Serves 6.

1 serving: 438 Calories; 12.2 g Total Fat; 483 mg Sodium; 23 g Protein; 60 g Carbohydrate; 5 g Dietary Fiber

Pictured on page 107.

TUNA BAKE SALAD

Just the right tang from the salad dressing.

Water	1 cup	250 mL
Skim evaporated milk	13½ oz.	385 mL
Light salad dressing (or mayonnaise)	¾ cup	175 mL
White vinegar	1 tbsp.	15 mL
Worcestershire sauce	1½ tsp.	7 mL
Cayenne pepper	⅛ tsp.	0.5 mL
Salt	1 tsp.	5 mL
Pepper	¼ tsp.	1 mL
Uncooked ditali (or elbow macaroni)	2 cups	500 mL
Finely chopped onion	½ cup	125 mL
Diced celery	¾ cup	175 mL
Grated carrot	½ cup	125 mL
Canned solid white tuna, drained and flaked	6½ oz.	184 g
Hard margarine (or butter)	2 tbsp.	30 mL
Dry bread crumbs	½ cup	125 mL

Whisk first 8 ingredients together in large bowl.

Add next 5 ingredients. Stir. Turn into ungreased 3 quart (3 L) casserole, making sure pasta is covered. Bake, uncovered, in 350°F (175°C) oven for 45 minutes. Stir well.

Melt margarine in small saucepan. Stir in bread crumbs. Sprinkle over top. Return to oven. Bake, uncovered, for 15 minutes until browned and pasta is tender but firm. Makes 7 cups (1.75 L).

1½ cups (375 mL): 517 Calories; 17.6 g Total Fat; 1309 mg Sodium; 23 g Protein; 66 g Carbohydrate; 2 g Dietary Fiber

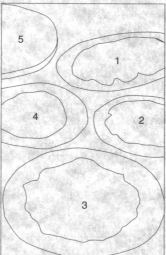

1. Chicken Caesar Salad, page 131
2. Sandwich Salad, page 132
3. Spicy Beef Salad, page 134
4. Rice And Bean Salad, page 132
5. Chicken Salad Pizza, page 129

Makes a light summer lunch or supper.

Hard margarine (or butter)	2 tsp.	10 mL
Boneless, skinless chicken breast halves (about 2), pounded flat	½ lb.	225 g
Reserved flavor packet		
Grated cabbage, lightly packed	4 cups	1 L
Package chicken-flavored instant noodles, flavor packet reserved	3 oz.	85 g
Toasted sesame seed	¼ cup	60 mL
Chopped green onion	¼ cup	60 mL
Grated carrot	½ cup	125 mL
DRESSING		
Water	½ cup	125 mL
Cornstarch	1 tbsp.	15 mL
Granulated sugar	2 tbsp.	30 mL
Salt	1 tsp.	5 mL
Pepper	¼ tsp.	1 mL
White vinegar	3 tbsp.	50 mL
Cooking oil	1 tbsp.	15 mL

Melt margarine in large frying pan. Brown 1 side of chicken in margarine. Turn. Sprinkle with contents of flavor packet. Brown second side until no longer pink. Cut into small cubes. Cool.

Place next 5 ingredients in large bowl. Add chicken.

Dressing: Combine water and cornstarch in small saucepan. Heat and stir until boiling and thickened. Remove from heat.

Add sugar, salt, pepper, vinegar and cooking oil. Stir until sugar is dissolved. Cool thoroughly. Pour over salad. Toss to coat. Chill. Serves 4.

1 serving: 294 Calories; 15 g Total Fat; 1139 mg Sodium; 17 g Protein; 24 g Carbohydrate; 4 g Dietary Fiber

CHICKEN AND RICE SALAD

Makes a very tasty light lunch or supper.

Boneless, skinless chicken breast halves (about 2), pounded flat	½ lb.	225 g
Cooking oil	1 tsp.	5 mL
Salt, sprinkle		
Pepper, sprinkle		
Uncooked long grain white rice	¾ cup	175 mL
Chopped onion	½ cup	125 mL
Chicken bouillon powder	2 tsp.	10 mL
Water	1½ cups	375 mL
Frozen peas	2 cups	500 mL
Water	½ cup	125 mL
Light salad dressing (or mayonnaise)	⅔ cup	150 mL
Milk	3 tbsp.	50 mL
White vinegar	1 tsp.	5 mL
Prepared mustard	½ tsp.	2 mL
Granulated sugar	½ tsp.	2 mL
Jar of chopped pimiento, drained	2 oz.	57 mL
Green onions, chopped	2	2
Small head of iceberg lettuce, cut or torn	1	1

Brown both sides of chicken in cooking oil in large frying pan. Sprinkle with salt and pepper. Cook until no longer pink. Cool. Cut into bite-size pieces.

Combine rice, onion, bouillon powder and first amount of water in medium saucepan. Cover. Simmer for 15 to 20 minutes until rice is tender and water is absorbed. Set saucepan, uncovered, in cold water in sink, stirring often, until cooled.

Cook peas in second amount of water in small saucepan until barely cooked. Drain. Rinse in cold water. Drain well. Put chicken, rice mixture and peas into large bowl.

Stir next 7 ingredients together in small bowl. Add to chicken mixture. Toss to coat.

Divide lettuce among 6 plates. Spoon chicken mixture over each. Serves 6.

1 serving: 287 Calories; 9.1 g Total Fat; 524 mg Sodium; 15 g Protein; 36 g Carbohydrate; 4 g Dietary Fiber

Wonderful fresh flavor. Serve with a knife and fork for easier eating. Assemble shortly before serving to prevent sogginess.

Partially baked commercial (12 inch, 30 cm) pizza crust	1	1
Light salad dressing (or mayonnaise)	½ cup	125 mL
Granulated sugar	½ tsp.	2 mL
Prepared mustard	½ tsp.	2 mL
Diced cooked chicken	1 cup	250 mL
Large hard-boiled eggs, chopped	2	2
Small red onion, thinly sliced (raw or cooked)	1	1
Sweet pickle relish	1 tbsp.	15 mL
Chopped celery	½ cup	125 mL
Salt	¼ tsp.	1 mL
Finely chopped lettuce, lightly packed	1½ cups	375 mL

Place crust on greased 12 inch (30 cm) pizza pan. Bake on bottom rack in 425°F (220°C) oven for 8 to 10 minutes until crisp. Cool.

Stir next 3 ingredients together in small bowl. Spread over crust.

Stir next 6 ingredients together in medium bowl.

Spread lettuce over salad dressing mixture on crust. Spoon dabs of chicken mixture here and there to cover. Cuts into 8 wedges.

1 wedge: 256 Calories; 9.8 g Total Fat; 340 mg Sodium; 11 g Protein; 30 g Carbohydrate; 2 g Dietary Fiber

Pictured on page 125.

Paré Pointer

Timbuktu can be found between Timbuk-one and Timbuk-three.

CHEF'S SALAD

Variation of an old standby. Yummy two ingredient dressing.

Cut or torn romaine lettuce	3 cups	750 mL
Cut or torn iceberg lettuce	3 cups	750 mL
Julienned cooked turkey (or chicken)	1 cup	250 mL
Chopped green onion	½ cup	125 mL
Julienned cooked beef (or ham)	1 cup	250 mL
Medium green pepper, cut julienne	½	½
Julienned Swiss (or your favorite) cheese	1 cup	250 mL
Pitted ripe (or pimiento-stuffed green) olives (1 or 2 per serving), optional	6-12	6-12
Large hard-boiled eggs, sliced	3	3
Medium tomatoes, diced	2	2
Large fresh mushrooms, sliced	6	6
DRESSING		
Light salad dressing (or mayonnaise)	⅔ cup	150 mL
Chili sauce	2 tbsp.	30 mL

Combine first 7 ingredients in large bowl. Divide among 6 plates.

Arrange olives, egg slices, tomato and mushrooms over each.

Dressing: Mix salad dressing and chili sauce in small cup. Drizzle over salad. Makes ¾ cup (175 mL). Serves 6.

1 serving: 298 Calories; 16.8 g Total Fat; 411 mg Sodium; 25 g Protein; 12 g Carbohydrate; 2 g Dietary Fiber

Pictured on page 71.

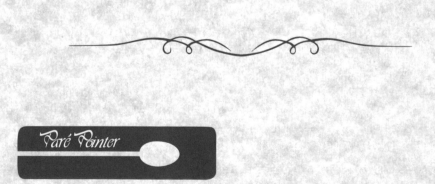

Paré Pointer

The pen is still mightier than the sword. No one has invented a ball point sword yet.

Chicken can be cooked ahead and served cold, or can be warmed before serving. Try the variation.

Large head of romaine lettuce, cut or torn	1	1
Croutons	½ cup	125 mL
Grated Parmesan cheese	2 tbsp.	30 mL
Hard margarine (or butter)	1 tsp.	5 mL
Boneless, skinless chicken breast halves (about 1 lb., 454 g), pounded flat	4	4
Salt, sprinkle		
Pepper, sprinkle		
Commercial light Creamy Caesar dressing	½ cup	125 mL
Granulated sugar (optional)	¼ tsp.	1 mL

Toss lettuce, croutons and cheese together in large bowl.

Melt margarine in large frying pan. Add chicken. Brown both sides. Sprinkle with salt and pepper. Cook until no longer pink.

Mix Caesar dressing and sugar in small cup. Pour over lettuce mixture. Toss together to coat. Divide among 4 plates. Cut each chicken breast into pieces or leave whole. Divide among salads, either over top or along side. Serves 4.

1 serving: 282 Calories; 13.2 g Total Fat; 389 mg Sodium; 31 g Protein; 9 g Carbohydrate; 2 g Dietary Fiber

Pictured on page 125.

Variation: Sprinkle chicken with seasoned salt, no-salt spice mix or lemon pepper.

Paré Pointer

The robot went berserk. They found he had a screw loose.

SANDWICH SALAD

Lots of flavor and lots of variety. A sandwich in a bowl.

Boneless, skinless chicken breast halves (about 2)	½ lb.	225 g
Cooking oil	1 tsp.	5 mL
Small head of lettuce, cut or torn	1	1
Chopped cooked ham	1 cup	250 mL
Green onions, chopped	2	2
Medium tomatoes, seeded and cut bite size	2	2
Large hard-boiled eggs, cut up	2	2
Cooked peas	1 cup	250 mL
Sliced cucumber (or sliced fresh mushrooms, pea pods, bean sprouts or chopped green or red pepper)	¾ cup	175 mL
Light salad dressing (or mayonnaise)	⅓ cup	75 mL
Chili sauce	1 tbsp.	15 mL

Cook chicken in cooking oil in large frying pan until no longer pink. Cut into bite-size pieces. Place in large bowl.

Add lettuce, ham, green onion, tomato, egg, peas and cucumber.

Stir salad dressing and chili sauce together in small cup. Pour over salad. Toss to coat. Makes 10 cups (2.5 L).

2 cups (500 mL): 233 Calories; 9.9 g Total Fat; 657 mg Sodium; 22 g Protein; 13 g Carbohydrate; 3 g Dietary Fiber

Pictured on page 125.

RICE AND BEAN SALAD

Makes lots of colorful salad.

Long grain white rice	1¼ cups	300 mL
Chopped onion	½ cup	125 mL
Boiling water	2½ cups	625 mL
Frozen kernel corn, thawed	1¼ cups	300 mL
Canned kidney beans, drained	14 oz.	398 mL
Chopped green onion	¼ cup	60 mL
Large tomato, seeded and diced	1	1
Light Italian dressing	1 cup	250 mL
Chili powder	1 tsp.	5 mL

(continued on next page)

Combine rice, onion and boiling water in medium saucepan. Cover. Simmer for about 15 to 20 minutes until rice is tender and water is absorbed. Cool.

Combine corn, beans, green onion and tomato in large bowl. Add rice mixture. Stir together.

Add Italian dressing. Sprinkle with chili powder. Stir well. Makes 9 cups (2.25 L).

1¹/₂ cups (375 mL): 258 Calories; 2.2 g Total Fat; 696 mg Sodium; 8 g Protein; 53 g Carbohydrate; 5 g Dietary Fiber

Pictured on page 125.

BEEF SALAD

Fresh tasting, dilly and creamy.

Julienned cooked roast beef	2 cups	500 mL
Chopped peeled cucumber	1 cup	250 mL
Radishes, sliced or diced	6	6
Chopped celery	¹/₂ cup	125 mL
Cooked peas	1 cup	250 mL
Cut or torn lettuce, lightly packed	4 cups	1 L
DRESSING		
Fat-free sour cream	1 cup	250 mL
Dill weed	1 tsp.	5 mL
Salt	¹/₂ tsp.	2 mL
Milk	1 tbsp.	15 mL
Granulated sugar	¹/₂ tsp.	2 mL

Combine first 6 ingredients in large bowl.

Dressing: Combine all 5 ingredients in small bowl. Chill for at least 30 minutes. Pour over salad just before serving. Toss to coat. Serves 4.

1 serving: 195 Calories; 4.3 g Total Fat; 476 mg Sodium; 26 g Protein; 13 g Carbohydrate; 3 g Dietary Fiber

SPICY BEEF SALAD

Apt to remind you of Szechuan beef. Delicious salad.

SUPREME DRESSING		
Light salad dressing (or mayonnaise)	½ cup	125 mL
Milk	¼ cup	60 mL
Prepared horseradish	1 tbsp.	15 mL
Chili sauce (or ketchup)	2 tsp.	10 mL
Granulated sugar	1 tsp.	5 mL
Onion powder	¼ tsp.	1 mL
MARINADE		
Soy sauce	2 tbsp.	30 mL
Water	2 tbsp.	30 mL
White vinegar	2 tbsp.	30 mL
Brown sugar, packed	3 tbsp.	50 mL
Worcestershire sauce	1 tsp.	5 mL
Dry mustard	½ tsp.	2 mL
Dried crushed chilies	½ tsp.	2 mL
Ground ginger	¼ tsp.	1 mL
Garlic powder	¼ tsp.	1 mL
Pepper	¼ tsp.	1 mL
Beef sirloin steak (partially frozen for easier slicing), cut into thin slices	1 lb.	454 g
Cooking oil	2 tsp.	10 mL
Cut or torn lettuce, lightly packed	5 cups	1.25 L
Chopped fresh mushrooms	1 cup	250 mL
Green onions, chopped	3	3
Thin green, red or orange pepper strips	½ cup	125 mL
Paper-thin red onion slices	⅓ cup	75 mL

Supreme Dressing: Stir all 6 ingredients together in small bowl. Makes ¾ cup (175 mL).

Marinade: Stir all 10 ingredients together in medium bowl.

Add beef to marinade. Stir to coat. Cover. Refrigerate for 2 to 3 hours.

Heat cooking oil in large frying pan. Drain beef well. Add to frying pan. Stir-fry until desired doneness.

(continued on next page)

Combine lettuce, mushrooms, green onion, green pepper strips and red onion in large bowl. Add 1 tbsp. (15 mL) dressing. Toss to coat. Divide among 4 plates. Spoon beef over each. Drizzle with remaining dressing or serve on the side. Serves 4.

1 serving: 323 Calories; 13.9 g Total Fat; 892 mg Sodium; 26 g Protein; 24 g Carbohydrate; 2 g Dietary Fiber

Pictured on page 125.

TACO SALAD

Quick and easy. Most can be prepared ahead to assemble just before serving. An interesting salad. Sour cream makes the perfect garnish.

Cooking oil	2 tsp.	10 mL
Lean ground beef	1 lb.	454 g
Chopped onion	1 cup	250 mL
Envelope taco seasoning mix	1 × 1¼ oz.	1 × 35 g
Canned tomatoes, with juice, broken up	14 oz.	398 mL
Grated light sharp Cheddar cheese	1 cup	250 mL
Cut or torn lettuce	6 cups	1.5 L
Medium tomatoes, diced	2	2
Grated light medium or sharp Cheddar cheese	½ cup	125 mL
Green onions, chopped	2	2
Tortilla chips, broken up	½ cup	125 mL

Heat cooking oil in large frying pan. Add ground beef and onion. Scramble-fry until onion is soft and beef is no longer pink. Drain.

Add taco seasoning mix, tomatoes with juice and first amount of cheese. Heat and stir until cheese is melted. Can prepare ahead to this point. Reheat before serving.

Divide lettuce among 6 plates. Scatter diced tomato over each. Spoon hot beef mixture over top. Sprinkle with second amount of cheese. Scatter green onion and tortilla chips over top. Serve immediately. Serves 6.

1 serving: 304 Calories; 16.5 g Total Fat; 997 mg Sodium; 24 g Protein; 16 g Carbohydrate; 3 g Dietary Fiber

Pictured on page 89.

TERIYAKI BEEF AND RICE SALAD

They're all here—hot, cold, sweet and sour.

Water	3 cups	750 mL
Lemon juice	¼ cup	60 mL
Soy sauce	2 tbsp.	30 mL
Brown sugar, packed	¼ cup	60 mL
Vegetable bouillon powder	2 tsp.	10 mL
Ground ginger	1 tsp.	5 mL
Pepper	¼ tsp.	1 mL
Garlic cloves, minced (or ½ tsp., 2 mL, powder)	2	2
Uncooked converted long grain white rice	1⅔ cups	400 mL
Sliced fresh mushrooms	2 cups	500 mL
Broccoli florets and thinly sliced stems	3 cups	750 mL
Cooked leftover (or deli) roast beef, cut into thin strips (about ½ lb., 225 g)	2 cups	500 mL
Cherry tomatoes, halved	12	12
Shredded lettuce	6 cups	1.5 L
Green onions, sliced	2	2

Measure first 10 ingredients into large saucepan. Stir together. Cover. Cook for about 15 minutes.

Stir in broccoli. Cover. Cook for 5 to 10 minutes until rice and broccoli are tender.

Stir in beef and tomato. Heat through.

Serve over lettuce. Sprinkle with green onion. Serves 6.

1 serving: 346 Calories; 2.9 g Total Fat; 599 mg Sodium; 18 g Protein; 62 g Carbohydrate; 4 g Dietary Fiber

Paré Pointer

To know how many feet are in a yard you have to find out how many people are standing in it.

Making this attractive soup is time-consuming but worth it. The tiny meatballs look really nice in the soup.

Canned tomatoes, with juice, broken up	14 oz.	398 mL
Chopped celery	½ cup	125 mL
Chopped onion	1¼ cups	300 mL
Medium potato, peeled and diced	1	1
Beef bouillon powder	2 tbsp.	30 mL
Water	6 cups	1.5 L
Garlic powder	¼ tsp.	1 mL
Parsley flakes	1 tsp.	5 mL
Salt	½ tsp.	2 mL
Granulated sugar	½ tsp.	2 mL
Dried sweet basil	½ tsp.	2 mL
Pepper	⅛ tsp.	0.5 mL
MEATBALLS		
Dry bread crumbs	¼ cup	60 mL
Salt	¼ tsp.	1 mL
Pepper	⅛ tsp.	0.5 mL
Seasoned salt	¼ tsp.	1 mL
Lean ground beef	½ lb.	225 g

Combine first 12 ingredients in large pot or Dutch oven. Stir together. Bring to a boil. Simmer, uncovered, for 30 minutes.

Meatballs: Mix bread crumbs, salt, pepper and seasoned salt in medium bowl. Add ground beef. Mix well. Shape into ½ inch (12 mm) balls. Arrange on greased baking sheet. Bake in 375°F (190°C) oven for 5 to 7 minutes. Add to pot. Simmer for 15 minutes. Makes 10½ cups (2.6 L).

2 cups (500 mL): 176 Calories; 7.4 g Total Fat; 1342 mg Sodium; 11 g Protein; 17 g Carbohydrate; 2 g Dietary Fiber

Paré Pointer

The toughest part of dieting is watching what your friends eat.

CHICKEN NOODLE SOUP

Flavorful with lots of noodles.

Cooking oil	2 tsp.	10 mL
Boneless, skinless chicken breast halves (about 3), pounded flat and cut bite size	¾ lb.	340 g
Cooking oil	2 tsp.	10 mL
Chopped onion	1½ cups	375 mL
Chopped celery	½ cup	125 mL
Thinly sliced carrot	1½ cups	375 mL
Salt	½ tsp.	2 mL
Pepper	¼ tsp.	1 mL
Ground thyme	⅛ tsp.	0.5 mL
Chicken bouillon powder	2 tbsp.	30 mL
Bay leaf	1	1
Parsley flakes	1 tsp.	5 mL
Water	6 cups	1.5 L
Uncooked broad egg noodles	3 cups	750 mL

Heat first amount of cooking oil in large frying pan. Add chicken. Brown and cook until no longer pink. Remove to large saucepan or pot.

Heat second amount of cooking oil in same frying pan. Add onion, celery and carrot. Stir-fry until tender-crisp. Add to saucepan.

Add remaining 8 ingredients. Bring to a boil. Boil gently for 8 to 9 minutes until pasta is tender but firm. Discard bay leaf. Makes 7½ cups (1.8 L).

2 cups (500 mL): 268 Calories; 7.7 g Total Fat; 1498 mg Sodium; 26 g Protein; 24 g Carbohydrate; 3 g Dietary Fiber

SPLIT PEA SOUP

Try this different version containing hot Italian sausage and potato.

Water	8 cups	2 L
Dried green split peas	2 cups	500 mL
Hot Italian sausages	½ lb.	225 g
Diced potato	1½ cups	375 mL
Diced or sliced carrot	1 cup	250 mL
Chopped onion	1 cup	250 mL
Chopped celery	½ cup	125 mL

(continued on next page)

Measure water and split peas into large pot or Dutch oven. Bring to a boil. Simmer, uncovered, stirring occasionally, for 1 hour.

Cook sausages in medium frying pan until well browned. Drain. Slice each sausage lengthwise into quarters. Cut into $1/4$ inch (6 mm) pieces. Add sausage pieces to pea mixture.

Add potato, carrot, onion and celery. Stir. Simmer, uncovered, stirring occasionally, for 40 minutes. Makes about 10 cups (2.5 L).

2 cups (500 mL): 426 Calories; 6.6 g Total Fat; 231 mg Sodium; 27 g Protein; 67 g Carbohydrate; 13 g Dietary Fiber

BEEF AND BARLEY SOUP

A meaty and filling soup.

Beef stew meat, trimmed of fat, diced into $1/4$ inch (6 mm) pieces	$3/4$ lb.	340 g
Pearl (or pot) barley	$1/3$ cup	75 mL
Canned tomatoes, with juice, broken up	14 oz.	398 mL
Liquid gravy browner	1 tsp.	5 mL
Water	7 cups	1.75 L
Finely shredded cabbage	1 cup	250 mL
Thinly sliced carrot	$1/2$ cup	125 mL
Thinly sliced celery	$1/2$ cup	125 mL
Chopped onion	1 cup	250 mL
Diced yellow turnip (rutabaga)	$1/2$ cup	125 mL
Beef bouillon powder	1 tbsp.	15 mL
Salt	$1/2$ tsp.	2 mL
Pepper	$1/4$ tsp.	1 mL
Parsley flakes	$1/2$ tsp.	2 mL
Dried sweet basil	$1/2$ tsp.	2 mL

Combine beef, barley, tomatoes with juice, gravy browner and water in large pot or Dutch oven. Simmer, uncovered, for 1 hour. Skim off foam as needed.

Add remaining 10 ingredients. Stir. Simmer, uncovered, stirring occasionally, for about 40 minutes. Makes $6^1/2$ cups (1.6 L).

2 cups (500 mL): 254 Calories; 4.3 g Total Fat; 1299 mg Sodium; 22 g Protein; 33 g Carbohydrate; 7 g Dietary Fiber

Pictured on page 143.

BLACK BEAN SOUP

Mild and so healthy. A sticks-to-the ribs soup.

Dried black beans	2 cups	500 mL
Water	12 cups	3 L
Chopped onion	2 cups	500 mL
Medium carrots, diced	2	2
Chopped celery	⅔ cup	150 mL
Lean ground beef	½ lb.	225 g
Chopped cooked ham	1¼ cups	300 mL
Garlic powder	¼ tsp.	1 mL
Brown sugar, packed	1 tbsp.	15 mL
Salt	1½ tsp.	7 mL
Pepper	¼ tsp.	1 mL
Dried sweet basil	1 tsp.	5 mL
Sherry (or alcohol-free sherry)	½ cup	125 mL
Chopped green onion	¼ cup	60 mL
Large hard-boiled eggs, grated	2	2
Freshly ground pepper, sprinkle		

Put beans into large pot or Dutch oven. Add water. Bring to a boil. Cover. Boil gently, stirring occasionally, for about 1¼ hours. Beans should be almost tender.

Add onion, carrot and celery. Cover. Boil gently for 30 minutes until tender.

Scramble-fry ground beef in medium non-stick frying pan until no longer pink. Drain. Add to beans.

Add next 6 ingredients. Stir. Run through blender to purée. Return to pot.

Add sherry. Stir. Heat through.

Sprinkle each serving with green onion and egg. Sprinkle pepper over top. Makes 14 cups (3.5 L).

2 cups (500 mL): *206 Calories; 5.7 g Total Fat; 1066 mg Sodium; 17 g Protein; 19 g Carbohydrate; 3 g Dietary Fiber*

Pictured on page 143.

A good substantial soup. Easy to make for a rainy day meal—or any day.

Cooking oil	1 tbsp.	15 mL
Lean ground beef	1 lb.	454 g
Chopped onion	1½ cups	375 mL
Chopped celery	1½ cups	375 mL
Grated carrot	¾ cup	175 mL
Canned kidney beans, with liquid	14 oz.	398 mL
Canned tomatoes, with juice, broken up	14 oz.	398 mL
Water	4 cups	1 L
Beef bouillon powder	4 tsp.	20 mL
Salt	1 tsp.	5 mL
Pepper	¼ tsp.	1 mL
Garlic powder	¼ tsp.	1 mL
Dried whole oregano	½ tsp.	2 mL
Dried sweet basil	½ tsp.	2 mL
Coarsely grated cabbage	3 cups	750 mL
Uncooked tiny shell pasta	¾ cup	175 mL
Grated Parmesan cheese, sprinkle		

Heat cooking oil in large frying pan. Add ground beef, onion, celery and carrot. Sauté until beef is no longer pink. Drain. Turn into large pot or Dutch oven.

Add next 9 ingredients. Stir together. Heat until boiling.

Add cabbage and pasta. Boil slowly, uncovered, stirring occasionally, for 20 minutes.

Serve with a sprinkle of cheese. Makes 12 cups (3 L).

2 cups (500 mL): 274 Calories; 8.3 g Total Fat; 1117 mg Sodium; 21 g Protein; 30 g Carbohydrate; 6 g Dietary Fiber

Pictured on page 53.

Paré Pointer

To make a sandcastle in a hurry, use quick sand.

HAM AND BEAN SOUP

A wonderful warm, comforting soup.

Dried navy beans	2 cups	500 mL
Lean meaty ham bone (or 2 smoked pork hocks)	1	1
Water	11 cups	2.75 L
Diced carrot	1 cup	250 mL
Chopped onion	1¼ cups	300 mL
Chopped celery	½ cup	125 mL
Salt	1½ tsp.	7 mL
Pepper	¼ tsp.	1 mL

Combine beans and ham bone in water in large pot or Dutch oven. Simmer, covered, for 1 hour until beans are almost tender. Remove ham bone. Skim off fat. Dice ham and return to pot.

Add remaining 5 ingredients. Stir together. Simmer for about 20 minutes until vegetables are tender. Makes 11 cups (2.75 L).

2 cups (500 mL): 316 Calories; 2.2 g Total Fat; 1118 mg Sodium; 24 g Protein; 52 g Carbohydrate; 8 g Dietary Fiber

Variation: Omit ham bone or pork hocks. Add 1 cup (250 mL) chopped cooked ham after beans have been cooked for 1 hour.

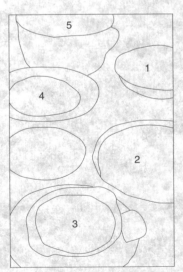

1. Chicken Rice Soup, page 145
2. Bouillabaisse, page 148
3. Spicy Fish Stewp, page 60
4. Beef And Barley Soup, page 139
5. Black Bean Soup, page 140

Props Courtesy Of: Dansk Gifts, Eaton's, Handworks Gallery, Le Gnome, Scona Clayworks, X/S Wares

At last, chicken soup with lots of chicken.

Boneless, skinless chicken breast halves (about 2)	½ lb.	225 g
Whole chicken legs (drumstick and thigh each), skin removed	2	2
Small bay leaf	1	1
Vegetable bouillon powder	1 tbsp.	15 mL
Water	6 cups	1.5 L
Chopped celery	1 cup	250 mL
Medium carrot, diced	1	1
Chopped onion	1½ cups	375 mL
Canned tomatoes, with juice, broken up	2 × 14 oz.	2 × 398 mL
Salt	½ tsp.	2 mL
Pepper, sprinkle		
Uncooked long grain white rice	½ cup	125 mL
Parsley flakes	1 tsp.	5 mL

Combine chicken, bay leaf and bouillon powder in water in large pot or Dutch oven. Bring to a boil. Skim off foam. Cook, uncovered, for about 30 minutes until chicken is tender. Remove chicken. Discard bones and bay leaf. Cut chicken into bite-size pieces. Return to pot.

Add next 6 ingredients. Cook, uncovered, for 20 minutes.

Add rice and parsley. Cook for 15 to 20 minutes until rice is tender. Makes 8½ cups (2.1 L).

2 cups (500 mL): 295 Calories; 4 g Total Fat; 1171 mg Sodium; 29 g Protein; 35 g Carbohydrate; 4 g Dietary Fiber

Pictured on page 143.

Paré Pointer

Their teacher is a regular bird. He watches them like a hawk.

CORN CHOWDER

Serve this for rave reviews.

Diced potato	3 cups	750 mL
Chopped celery	1 cup	250 mL
Grated carrot	1 cup	250 mL
Chopped onion	1 cup	250 mL
Water	1 cup	250 mL
Diced bacon	1 cup	250 mL
Milk	2¼ cups	560 mL
All-purpose flour	¼ cup	60 mL
Skim evaporated milk	13½ oz.	385 mL
Salt	1 tsp.	5 mL
Pepper	½ tsp.	2 mL
Canned cream-style corn	14 oz.	398 mL

Cook potato, celery, carrot and onion slowly in water in large pot or Dutch oven until tender. Add a bit more water, if necessary, to keep from burning. Remove to large bowl.

Cook bacon in medium frying pan until crispy. Drain. Add to cooked vegetables.

Gradually whisk both milks together into flour, salt and pepper in small bowl. Add to pot. Heat and stir until boiling and thickened.

Add corn and vegetable mixture. Stir. Heat through. Makes 10 cups (2.5 L).

2 cups (500 mL): *419 Calories; 12 g Total Fat; 1303 mg Sodium; 21 g Protein; 59 g Carbohydrate; 4 g Dietary Fiber*

Pictured on page 89.

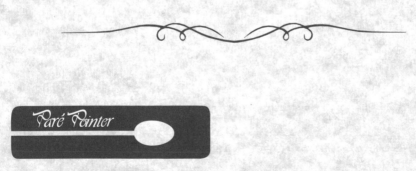

There is no better or more blessed bondage than to be a prisoner of hope.

This has a mild curry flavor. If you're into the real thing you will want to double the curry powder.

Boneless, skinless chicken breast halves (about 2)	1/2 lb.	225 g
Dried yellow split peas	1/3 cup	75 mL
Boiling water	8 cups	2 L
Hard margarine (or butter)	2 tbsp.	30 mL
Chopped onion	1 1/2 cups	375 mL
Large cooking apple, peeled and diced (McIntosh is good)	1	1
Curry powder	1 tbsp.	15 mL
All-purpose flour	1/4 cup	60 mL
Salt	1/2 tsp.	2 mL
Pepper	1/8 tsp.	0.5 mL
Diced carrot	2/3 cup	150 mL
Diced celery	2/3 cup	150 mL
Ground mace	1/8 tsp.	0.5 mL
Ground cloves	1/8 tsp.	0.5 mL
Canned tomatoes, with juice, broken up	14 oz.	398 mL
Skim evaporated milk	1 cup	250 mL
Cooked long grain white rice (optional), allow 1/4 cup (60 mL) per bowl		

Combine chicken and split peas in boiling water in large pot or Dutch oven. Cover. Boil gently for about 10 minutes until chicken is tender. Skim off foam. Remove chicken to plate. Dice. Return to pot.

Melt margarine in large frying pan. Add onion, apple and curry powder. Sauté for about 5 minutes until onion is soft.

Mix in flour, salt and pepper. Stir into chicken mixture.

Add carrot, celery, mace, cloves and tomatoes with juice. Simmer, uncovered, for 30 to 40 minutes until carrot is tender.

Stir in evaporated milk. Heat through.

Scoop 1/4 cup (60 mL) of rice into each soup bowl. Fill with soup. Makes 9 cups (2.25 L).

2 cups (500 mL): 301 Calories; 6.9 g Total Fat; 638 mg Sodium; 23 g Protein; 38 g Carbohydrate; 6 g Dietary Fiber

BOUILLABAISSE

Pronounced BOOL-yuh-BAYZ. Very well-known fish and seafood soup.

Olive (or cooking) oil	2 tsp.	10 mL
Garlic cloves, minced (or ½ tsp., 2 mL, powder)	2	2
Finely diced onion	½ cup	125 mL
Chopped celery, with leaves	1 cup	250 mL
Water	1 cup	250 mL
White (or alcohol-free white) wine	½ cup	125 mL
Canned stewed tomatoes, with juice, blended	14 oz.	398 mL
Medium green or yellow pepper, diced	1	1
Sweet potatoes, diced	12 oz.	341 mL
Granulated sugar	1 tsp.	5 mL
Salt	½ tsp.	2 mL
Dried sweet basil	1 tsp.	5 mL
Thyme leaves	½ tsp.	2 mL
Dried crushed chilies, finely crushed	⅛ tsp.	0.5 mL
Hot pepper sauce, just a dash		
Skim evaporated milk	1 cup	250 mL
All-purpose flour	1 tbsp.	15 mL
Seafood (or chicken) bouillon powder	2 tsp.	10 mL
Fresh (or frozen, partially thawed) cod fillets, cut into 1½ inch (3.8 cm) squares	1 lb.	454 g
Uncooked fresh (or frozen, thawed) medium shrimp, peeled and deveined	4 oz.	113 g
Frozen tiny (bay) scallops	4 oz.	113 g
Chopped fresh parsley, for garnish	2 tbsp.	30 mL

Heat olive oil in large pot or Dutch oven. Add garlic, onion and celery. Sauté until onion is soft.

Stir in next 11 ingredients. Bring to a boil. Cover. Simmer for 30 minutes until vegetables are tender.

Gradually whisk evaporated milk into flour and bouillon powder in small bowl. Stir into simmering mixture until boiling and thickened.

(continued on next page)

Add fish, shrimp and scallops. Cover. Cook gently for 6 to 10 minutes until fish flakes, shrimp curl and turn pink and scallops are opaque.

Garnish with parsley. Makes 9 cups (2.25 L).

2 cups (500 mL): 309 Calories; 3.9 g Total Fat; 1037 mg Sodium; 33 g Protein; 32 g Carbohydrate; 4 g Dietary Fiber

Pictured on page 143.

TUNA CORN CHOWDER

Depending on what you serve with this, you may want to double the recipe.

Bacon slices, diced	4	4
Chopped onion	1 cup	250 mL
Chopped green pepper	1/4 cup	60 mL
Medium carrot, diced	1	1
Medium potato, diced	1	1
Frozen kernel corn	1 cup	250 mL
All-purpose flour	1/4 cup	60 mL
Chicken bouillon powder	1 tsp.	5 mL
Salt	1/4 tsp.	1 mL
Pepper	1/4 tsp.	1 mL
Parsley flakes	1/2 tsp.	2 mL
Milk	5 cups	1.25 L
Instant potato flakes	1/4-1/2 cup	60-125 mL
Canned solid white tuna, drained and flaked	6 1/2 oz.	184 g

Put first 6 ingredients into large frying pan. Sauté until bacon is crispy. Cover most of the time so vegetables cook.

Mix in flour, bouillon powder, salt, pepper and parsley.

Stir in milk until boiling and thickened. Add potato flakes. Stir together until thickened.

Add tuna. Stir together. Heat through. Makes 6 cups (1.5 L).

2 cups (500 mL): 588 Calories; 24.1 g Total Fat; 1085 mg Sodium; 35 g Protein; 60 g Carbohydrate; 4 g Dietary Fiber

CREAMY FISH CHOWDER

Creamy with mild garlic flavor. A delicious hearty soup.

Hard margarine (or butter)	2 tsp.	10 mL
Finely chopped onion	½ cup	125 mL
Water	3 cups	750 mL
Seafood (or vegetable) bouillon powder	3 tbsp.	50 mL
Diced celery	1½ cups	375 mL
Small carrots, thinly sliced	1½ cups	375 mL
Medium potatoes, diced	2	2
Pepper	¼ tsp.	1 mL
Thyme leaves	¼ tsp.	1 mL
Bay leaves	2	2
Fresh (or frozen, thawed) cod fillets, cut into 1½ inch (3.8 cm) squares	1 lb.	454 g
Skim evaporated milk	⅔ cup	150 mL
All-purpose flour	¼ cup	60 mL
Chopped fresh parsley, for garnish		

Melt margarine in large pot or Dutch oven. Add onion. Sauté until soft.

Add next 8 ingredients. Stir together. Bring to a boil. Simmer, uncovered, for about 15 minutes until potato is tender. Discard bay leaves.

Gently stir in fish. Cover. Cook for about 5 minutes until fish flakes.

Gradually whisk evaporated milk into flour in small bowl until smooth. Stir slowly into chowder until boiling and thickened.

Sprinkle with parsley. Makes 8 cups (2 L).

2 cups (500 mL): 274 Calories; 3.8 g Total Fat; 1534 mg Sodium; 28 g Protein; 32 g Carbohydrate; 3 g Dietary Fiber

Paré Pointer

Turkeys don't eat much because they're always stuffed.

Throughout this book measurements are given in Conventional and Metric measure. To compensate for differences between the two measurements due to rounding, a full metric measure is not always used. The cup used is the standard 8 fluid ounce. Temperature is given in degrees Fahrenheit and Celsius. Baking pan measurements are in inches and centimetres as well as quarts and litres. An exact metric conversion is given below as well as the working equivalent (Standard Measure).

OVEN TEMPERATURES

Fahrenheit (°F)	Celsius (°C)
175°	80°
200°	95°
225°	110°
250°	120°
275°	140°
300°	150°
325°	160°
350°	175°
375°	190°
400°	205°
425°	220°
450°	230°
475°	240°
500°	260°

SPOONS

Conventional Measure	Metric Exact Conversion Millilitre (mL)	Metric Standard Measure Millilitre (mL)
1/8 teaspoon (tsp.)	0.6 mL	0.5 mL
1/4 teaspoon (tsp.)	1.2 mL	1 mL
1/2 teaspoon (tsp.)	2.4 mL	2 mL
1 teaspoon (tsp.)	4.7 mL	5 mL
2 teaspoons (tsp.)	9.4 mL	10 mL
1 tablespoon (tbsp.)	14.2 mL	15 mL

CUPS

	Metric Exact Conversion	Metric Standard Measure
1/4 cup (4 tbsp.)	56.8 mL	60 mL
1/3 cup (5 1/3 tbsp.)	75.6 mL	75 mL
1/2 cup (8 tbsp.)	113.7 mL	125 mL
2/3 cup (10 2/3 tbsp.)	151.2 mL	150 mL
3/4 cup (12 tbsp.)	170.5 mL	175 mL
1 cup (16 tbsp.)	227.3 mL	250 mL
4 1/2 cups	1022.9 mL	1000 mL (1 L)

PANS

Conventional Inches	Metric Centimetres
8x8 inch	20x20 cm
9x9 inch	22x22 cm
9x13 inch	22x33 cm
10x15 inch	25x38 cm
11x17 inch	28x43 cm
8x2 inch round	20x5 cm
9x2 inch round	22x5 cm
10x4 1/2 inch tube	25x11 cm
8x4x3 inch loaf	20x10x7.5 cm
9x5x3 inch loaf	22x12.5x7.5 cm

DRY MEASUREMENTS

Conventional Measure Ounces (oz.)	Metric Exact Conversion Grams (g)	Metric Standard Measure Grams (g)
1 oz.	28.3 g	28 g
2 oz.	56.7 g	57 g
3 oz.	85.0 g	85 g
4 oz.	113.4 g	125 g
5 oz.	141.7 g	140 g
6 oz.	170.1 g	170 g
7 oz.	198.4 g	200 g
8 oz.	226.8 g	250 g
16 oz.	453.6 g	500 g
32 oz.	907.2 g	1000 g (1 kg)

CASSEROLES (Canada & Britain)

Standard Size Casserole	Exact Metric Measure
1 qt. (5 cups)	1.13 L
1 1/2 qts. (7 1/2 cups)	1.69 L
2 qts. (10 cups)	2.25 L
2 1/2 qts. (12 1/2 cups)	2.81 L
3 qts. (15 cups)	3.38 L
4 qts. (20 cups)	4.5 L
5 qts. (25 cups)	5.63 L

CASSEROLES (United States)

Standard Size Casserole	Exact Metric Measure
1 qt. (4 cups)	900 mL
1 1/2 qts. (6 cups)	1.35 L
2 qts. (8 cups)	1.8 L
2 1/2 qts. (10 cups)	2.25 L
3 qts. (12 cups)	2.7 L
4 qts. (16 cups)	3.6 L
5 qts. (20 cups)	4.5 L

INDEX

Arroz Con Pollo 106
Autumn Bake 22

Baked Paella Casserole 109
Barley Soup, Beef And 139
Bean Dish 64
Beans
   Beef And Bean Stew 27
   Black Bean Soup 140
   Brunswick Stew 114
   Chicken And Black Bean Stew 100
   Comfort Chili 10
   Ham And Bean Soup 142
   Macaroni Hash 12
   Meatless Chili 62
   Mexican Corn Chip Casserole 21
   Minestrone 141
   Rice And Bean Salad 132
   Simple Cassoulet 81
   Three Bean Bake 23
   Wieners And 83
Beef (see also Ground Beef)
   Autumn Bake 22
   Borscht Stew 30
   Chef's Salad 130
   Corned Beef Bake 39
   Corny Beef Enchiladas 38
   Dilly Beef Dinner 24
   Dinty's Special 33
   Oven Stew 29
   Pot Roast 32
   Short Rib Dinner 37
   Spicy Beef Salad 134
   Steak in Foil 34
   Stove Top Pot Pie 26
   Teriyaki Beef And Rice Salad 136
   Veggie Beef Casserole 25
Beef And Barley Soup 139
Beef And Bean Stew 27
Beef And Dumplings 31
Beef Patties 13
Beef Salad 133
Beef Stewed In Wine 28
Beef Stroganoff 119
Beefy Rice Casserole 24
Biscuit Dumplings 31
Biscuit Topping 26
Black Bean Soup 140
Black Bean Stew, Chicken And 100
Borscht Stew 30
Bouillabaisse 148
Breakfast Strata 45
Broccoli Chicken, Rice And 111
Broccoli Ham Rolls 86

Broccoli Pie, Chicken 93
Brunswick Stew 114

Cabbage Casserole, Ham And 85
Cabbage Roll Casserole, Lazy 16
Caesar Salad, Chicken 131
Cappelletti Casserole 19
Cassoulet, Simple 81
Cheesy Rice Casserole 65
Cheesy Wieners And Potatoes 82
Chef's Salad 130
Chicken (see also Ground Chicken)
   Arroz Con Pollo 106
   Baked Paella Casserole 109
   Brunswick Stew 114
   Chef's Salad 130
   Curried Peanut 99
   Jambalaya 104
   Mulligatawny 147
   Quick Chicken Chow Mein 97
   Rice And Broccoli 111
   Roast Chicken Dinner 102
   Sandwich Salad 132
   Simple Chicken Bake 103
   Stuffing Crust Pie 117
   Sweet And Sour Skillet 98
   Vegetable 112
   Whiskey Stew 115
Chicken And Black Bean Stew 100
Chicken And Dumplings 110
Chicken And Jiffy Dumplings 113
Chicken And Rice Salad 128
Chicken Broccoli Pie 93
Chicken Caesar Salad 131
Chicken Fajita Dinner 96
Chicken Noodle Soup 138
Chicken Pot Au Feu 101
Chicken Rice Soup 145
Chicken Salad Pizza 129
Chicken Slaw 127
Chicken Strata 116
Chicken Stroganoff 119
Chicken Tetrazzini 95
Chicken Veronique 94
Chicken Vinaigrette 105
Chili
   Comfort 10
   Meatless 62
Chow Mein, Quick Chicken 97
Chowder
   Corn 146
   Creamy Fish 150
   Tuna Corn 149

Cole Slaw
  Chicken. 127
  Pasta 121
Comfort Chili 10
Corn Chowder 146
Corned Beef Bake 39
Corny Beef Enchiladas 38
Crab Casserole, Mushroom And 50
Crab Salad 120
Cranberry Rice, Turkey With. 118
Cream Sauce, Mushroom 87
Creamed Rice And Salmon 55
Creamy Fish Chowder 150
Curried Peanut Chicken 99
Curried Pork And Mango Sauce 76

Dilly Beef Dinner 24
Dinty's Special. 33
Dressing, Supreme 134
Dumplings 110
Dumplings
  Beef And 31
  Biscuit. 31
  Chicken And 110
  Chicken And Jiffy 113

Easy Taco Supper 11
Egg Scramble Deluxe 44
Eggs
  Breakfast Strata 45
  Chef's Salad 130
  Chicken Salad Pizza 129
  Chicken Strata 116
  Crab Salad 120
  Ham Stratawich 42
  Red-Topped Frittata 41
  Sandwich Salad 132
  Spinach Onion Quiche 43
  Zucchini Frittata 40
Enchiladas, Corny Beef 38

Fajita Dinner, Chicken 96
Fettuccine, Shrimp. 59
Fish & Seafood
  Baked Paella Casserole 109
  Bouillabaisse. 148
  Crab Salad 120
  Creamed Rice And Salmon. 55
  Creamy Fish Chowder. 150
  Jambalaya 104
  Mushroom And Crab Casserole . . . 50
  Neptune's Pie 51
  Pasta Slaw 121
  Quick Tuna Casserole 49

Salmon Stew 57
Scalloped Salmon 56
Shrimp Fettuccine 59
Shrimp Supreme 58
Spicy Fish Stewp 60
Standby Tuna Casserole 48
Tuna Bake Salad 124
Tuna Corn Chowder 149
Tuna Frills 46
Tuna Penne Salad 123
Tuna Potato Griddle 47
Fish Chowder, Creamy 150
Fish Fantastic 52
Frittata, Red-Topped 41
Frittata, Zucchini 40

Greek Pizza 75
Ground Beef
  Beef And Bean Stew 27
  Beef Patties 13
  Beef Stroganoff 119
  Beefy Rice Casserole 24
  Black Bean Soup 140
  Cappelletti Casserole 19
  Comfort Chili. 10
  Easy Taco Supper. 11
  Layered Casserole 15
  Lazy Cabbage Roll Casserole 16
  Macaroni Hash 12
  Meat And Potatoes 10
  Meatball Soup 137
  Meatballs 137
  Meatloaf Casserole 20
  Mexican Corn Chip Casserole 21
  Minestrone 141
  Oriental Beef Dinner 14
  Patty Bake 13
  Saucy Skillet Dinner 8
  Taco Salad 135
  Tamale Rice Dish 9
  Three Bean Bake 23
  Veggie Beef Casserole 25
Ground Chicken
  Chicken Broccoli Pie 93
  Chicken Strata 116
  Chicken Stroganoff 119
  Chicken Veronique 94
  Quick Chicken Stroganoff 92

Ham
  Black Bean Soup 140
  Broccoli Ham Rolls 86
  Chef's Salad 130
  Egg Scramble Deluxe 44

Jambalaya 104
  Pasta Ham Salad 122
  Pineapple Ham Bake 84
  Red-Topped Frittata 41
  Sandwich Salad 132
Ham And Bean Soup 142
Ham And Cabbage Casserole 85
Ham And Potatoes 84
Ham Stratawich 42
Ham Veggie Scallop 87
Hash, Macaroni 12
Hash, Sausage 78

Italian Pasta Skillet 80

Jambalaya 104

Lamb
  Moussaka 91
Lamb Stew 88
Layered Casserole 15
Lazy Cabbage Roll Casserole 16

Macaroni Hash 12
Macaroni Special 63
Mango Sauce 76
Mango Sauce, Curried Pork And 76
Meat And Potatoes 10
Meatball Soup 137
Meatballs 137
Meatless
  Bean Dish 64
  Cheesy Rice Casserole 65
  Macaroni Special 63
  Shells Primavera 61
Meatless Chili 62
Meatloaf Casserole 20
Mexican Corn Chip Casserole 21
Minestrone 141
Moussaka 91
Mulligatawny 147
Mushroom And Crab Casserole 50
Mushroom Cream Sauce 87

Neptune's Pie 51
Noodle Soup, Chicken 138
Noodles, Pork And 74

Onion Quiche, Spinach 43
Oriental Beef Dinner 14
Oven Stew 29

Paella Casserole, Baked 109
Pasta
  Beef Stewed In Wine 28

Beef Stroganoff 119
Broccoli Ham Rolls 86
Cappelletti Casserole 19
Chicken Noodle Soup 138
Chicken Stroganoff 119
Chicken Tetrazzini 95
Corned Beef Bake 39
Curried Pork And Mango Sauce . . . 76
Easy Taco Supper 11
Ham And Cabbage Casserole 85
Italian Pasta Skillet 80
Layered Casserole 15
Macaroni Hash 12
Macaroni Special 63
Minestrone 141
Mushroom And Crab Casserole 50
Pasta Slaw 121
Patty Bake 13
Pork And Noodles 74
Pork Stew With Rotini 66
Quick Chicken Stroganoff 92
Saucy Skillet Dinner 8
Shells Primavera 61
Shrimp Fettuccine 59
Simple Chicken Bake 103
Spicy Sausage And 79
Standby Tuna Casserole 48
Tuna Bake Salad 124
Tuna Frills 46
Tuna Penne Salad 123
Turkey Stroganoff 119
Veggie Beef Casserole 25
Pasta Ham Salad 122
Pasta Slaw 121
Patties, Beef 13
Patty Bake 13
Pea Soup, Split 138
Peanut Chicken, Curried 99
Penne Salad, Tuna 123
Pie
  Chicken Broccoli 93
  Chicken Veronique 94
  Neptune's 51
  Stove Top Pot 26
  Stuffing Crust 117
  Turkey Veronique 94
Pineapple Ham Bake 84
Pineapple Pork And Rice 73
Pizza, Chicken Salad 129
Pizza, Greek 75
Pork (see also Ham)
  Breakfast Strata 45
  Broccoli Ham Rolls 86
  Cheesy Wieners And Potatoes 82

Chef's Salad 130
Corn Chowder. 146
Curried Pork And Mango Sauce 76
Greek Pizza 75
Ham And Bean Soup 142
Ham And Cabbage Casserole. 85
Ham And Potatoes 84
Ham Stratawich 42
Ham Veggie Scallop 87
Italian Pasta Skillet 80
Jambalaya 104
Pasta Ham Salad 122
Pineapple Ham Bake 84
Pineapple Pork And Rice 73
Quick Fix Meal 70
Roast Chicken Dinner 102
Sandwich Salad 132
Sausage Hash 78
Simple Cassoulet 81
Spicy Sausage And Pasta. 79
Stir-Fry 69
Tuna Corn Chowder 149
Veggie Beef Casserole 25
Wieners And Beans 83
Pork And Noodles 74
Pork And Rice Dish 68
Pork Chop Dinner 67
Pork Stew 77
Pork Stew With Rotini 66
Pot Au Feu, Chicken 101
Pot Pie, Stove Top 26
Pot Roast 32
Primavera, Shells 61

Quiche, Spinach Onion 43
Quick Chicken Chow Mein. 97
Quick Chicken Stroganoff 92
Quick Fix Meal 70
Quick Tuna Casserole 49

Red-Topped Frittata. 41
Rib Dinner, Short. 37
Rice
    Arroz Con Pollo. 106
    Baked Paella Casserole 109
    Beefy Rice Casserole 24
    Cheesy Rice Casserole. 65
    Chicken And Rice Salad 128
    Chicken Pot Au Feu. 101
    Chicken Rice Soup 145
    Creamed Rice And Salmon. 55
    Curried Peanut Chicken 99
    Fish Fantastic 52
    Lazy Cabbage Roll Casserole 16

Mulligatawny 147
Oriental Beef Dinner 14
Pineapple Pork And 73
Pork And Rice Dish. 68
Quick Tuna Casserole 49
Sausage Hash 78
Shrimp Supreme. 58
Stir-Fry Pork 69
Sweet And Sour Skillet 98
Tamale Rice Dish 9
Teriyaki Beef And Rice Salad 136
Turkey With Cranberry. 118

Roast Chicken Dinner 102
Roast, Pot 32
Rotini, Pork Stew With 66

Salad
    Beef 133
    Chef's 130
    Chicken And Rice 128
    Chicken Caesar 131
    Chicken Salad Pizza 129
    Chicken Slaw 127
    Crab 120
    Pasta Ham 122
    Pasta Slaw 121
    Rice And Bean 132
    Sandwich 132
    Spicy Beef 134
    Taco 135
    Teriyaki Beef And Rice 136
    Tuna Bake. 124
    Tuna Penne. 123
Salmon, Creamed Rice And 55
Salmon, Scalloped. 56
Salmon Stew. 57
Sandwich Salad. 132
Sauce, Mango. 76
Sauce, Mushroom Cream 87
Saucy Skillet Dinner 8
Sausage Hash. 78
Sausage Stuffing. 102
Sausages
    Breakfast Strata 45
    Italian Pasta Skillet 80
    Roast Chicken Dinner 102
    Simple Cassoulet 81
    Spicy Sausage And Pasta. 79
    Split Pea Soup 138
Scalloped Salmon 56
Shells Primavera 61

Short Rib Dinner 37
Shrimp Fettuccine 59
Shrimp Supreme 58
Simple Cassoulet 81
Simple Chicken Bake 103
Slow Cooker
    Beefy Rice Casserole 24
    Dilly Beef Dinner 24
    Ham And Potatoes 84
    Meat And Potatoes 10
    Salmon Stew 57
Soup
    Beef And Barley 139
    Black Bean 140
    Bouillabaisse 148
    Chicken Noodle 138
    Chicken Rice 145
    Corn Chowder 146
    Creamy Fish Chowder 150
    Ham And Bean 142
    Meatball 137
    Minestrone 141
    Mulligatawny 147
    Spicy Fish Stewp 60
    Split Pea 138
    Tuna Corn Chowder 149
Spicy Beef Salad 134
Spicy Fish Stewp 60
Spicy Sausage And Pasta 79
Spinach Onion Quiche 43
Split Pea Soup 138
Standby Tuna Casserole 48
Steak In Foil 34
Stew
    Beef And Bean 27
    Borscht 30
    Brunswick 114
    Chicken And Black Bean 100
    Lamb 88
    Oven 29
    Pork 77
    Pork Stew With Rotini 66
    Salmon 57
    Spicy Fish Stewp 60
    Whiskey 115
Stir-Fry
    Chicken Fajita Dinner 96
    Curried Pork And Mango Sauce 76
    Pork And Noodles 74
    Quick Chicken Chow Mein 97
    Sweet And Sour Skillet 98
Stir-Fry Pork 69
Stove Top Pot Pie 26

Strata
    Breakfast 45
    Chicken 116
    Ham Stratawich 42
    Turkey 116
Stroganoff
    Beef 119
    Chicken 119
    Quick Chicken 92
    Turkey 119
Stuffing Crust Pie 117
Stuffing, Sausage 102
Supreme Dressing 134
Sweet And Sour Skillet 98

Taco Salad 135
Taco Supper, Easy 11
Tamale Rice Dish 9
Teriyaki Beef And Rice Salad 136
Tetrazzini, Chicken 95
Three Bean Bake 23
Tuna Bake Salad 124
Tuna Casserole, Quick 49
Tuna Casserole, Standby 48
Tuna Corn Chowder 149
Tuna Frills 46
Tuna Penne Salad 123
Tuna Potato Griddle 47
Turkey
    Chef's Salad 130
    Stuffing Crust Pie 117
Turkey Strata 116
Turkey Stroganoff 119
Turkey Veronique 94
Turkey With Cranberry Rice 118

Vegetable Chicken 112
Veggie Beef Casserole 25
Veggie Scallop, Ham 87

Whiskey Stew 115
Wieners And Beans 83
Wieners And Potatoes, Cheesy 82
Wine
    Beef Stewed In 28
    Chicken Veronique 94
    Jambalaya 104
    Rice And Broccoli Chicken 111
    Spicy Fish Stewp 60
    Turkey Veronique 94
    Vegetable Chicken 112

Zucchini Frittata 40

The Rookie Cook

New July 1, 2002

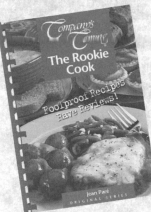

The Rookie Cook has easy-to-make, yet impressive, recipes that will build confidence in the beginner chef. Rave reviews are in the making!

Pecan Chip Cookies

Lots of pecans and chocolate chips in these delicious cookies.
Be sure not to overbake so they stay soft.

Hard margarine (or butter), softened	1 cup	250 mL
Brown sugar, packed	1 1/2 cups	375 mL
Granulated sugar	1/2 cup	125 mL
Large eggs	2	2
Vanilla	1 1/2 tsp.	7 mL
All-purpose flour	2 1/2 cups	625 mL
Baking powder	1 tsp.	5 mL
Baking soda	1 tsp.	5 mL
Salt	1/2 tsp.	2 mL
Semisweet chocolate chips	2 cups	500 mL
Chopped pecans	1 cup	250 mL

Cream margarine and both sugars together in large bowl until light and fluffy. Add eggs, 1 at a time, beating well after each addition. Add vanilla. Beat well.

Combine flour, baking powder, baking soda and salt in medium bowl. Add to margarine mixture. Mix until no dry flour remains and stiff dough forms.

Add chocolate chips and pecans. Stir until evenly distributed. Drop by tablespoonfuls, 2 to 3 inches (5 to 7.5 cm) apart, onto greased cookie sheets. Bake in 350°F (175°C) oven for 10 minutes until edges are golden. Do not overbake. Let stand on cookie sheets for 3 minutes before removing to wire racks to cool. Makes 7 dozen cookies.

1 cookie: 87 Calories; 4.7 g Total Fat; 64 mg Sodium; 1 g Protein; 11 g Carbohydrate; trace Dietary Fiber

Company's Coming cookbooks are available at retail locations throughout Canada!

See mail order offer on next page

Buy any 2 cookbooks—choose a 3rd FREE of equal or less value than the lowest price paid.

Original Series — CA$14.99 Canada — US$10.99 USA & International

CODE		CODE	
SQ	150 Delicious Squares	CT	Cooking For Two
CA	Casseroles	BB	Breakfasts & Brunches
MU	Muffins & More	SC	Slow Cooker Recipes
SA	Salads	ODM	One Dish Meals
AP	Appetizers	ST	Starters
DE	Desserts	SF	Stir-Fry
SS	Soups & Sandwiches	MAM	Make-Ahead Meals
CO	Cookies	PB	The Potato Book
MC	Main Courses	CCLFC	Low-Fat Cooking
PA	Pasta	CCLFP	Low-Fat Pasta
BA	Barbecues	AC	Appliance Cooking
LR	Light Recipes	CFK	Cook For Kids
PR	Preserves	SCH	Stews, Chilies & Chowders
LCA	Light Casseroles	FD	Fondues
CH	Chicken	CCBE	The Beef Book
KC	Kids Cooking	ASI	Asian Cooking
BR	Breads	CB	The Cheese Book
ME	Meatless Cooking	RC	The Rookie Cook ◀NEW▶ July 1/02

Greatest Hits — CA$12.99 Canada — US$9.99 USA & International

CODE		CODE	
BML	Biscuits, Muffins & Loaves	SAW	Sandwiches & Wraps
DSD	Dips, Spreads & Dressings	ITAL	Italian
SAS	Soups & Salads	MEX	Mexican

Lifestyle Series — CA$16.99 Canada — US$12.99 USA & International

CODE	
GR	Grilling
DC	Diabetic Cooking

Special Occasion Series — CA$19.99 Canada — US$19.99 USA & International

CODE		CODE	
CE	Chocolate Everything	CFS	Cooking for the Seasons
GFK	Gifts from the Kitchen		

Company's Coming COOKBOOKS®

www.companyscoming.com
visit our web-site

COMPANY'S COMING PUBLISHING LIMITED
2311 - 96 Street
Edmonton, Alberta, Canada T6N 1G3
Tel: (780) 450-6223 Fax: (780) 450-1857

Exclusive Mail Order Offer

See page 158 for list of cookbooks

Buy 2 Get 1 FREE!
Buy any 2 cookbooks—choose a 3rd FREE of equal or less value than the lowest price paid.

Quantity	Code	Title	Price Each	Price Total
			$	$
		don't forget		
		to indicate your		
		free book(s).		
		(see exclusive mail order		
		offer above)		
		please print		

TOTAL BOOKS (including FREE)

TOTAL BOOKS PURCHASED:

	International	Canada & USA
Plus Shipping & Handling (per destination)	$7.00 (one book)	$5.00 (1-3 books)
Additional Books (including FREE books)	$ ($2.00 each)	$ ($1.00 each)
Sub-Total	$	$
Canadian residents add G.S.T(7%)		$
TOTAL AMOUNT ENCLOSED	$	$

The Fine Print

- Orders outside Canada must be **PAID IN US FUNDS** by cheque or money order drawn on Canadian or US bank or by credit card.
- Make cheque or money order payable to: **COMPANY'S COMING PUBLISHING LIMITED**.
- Prices are expressed in Canadian dollars for Canada, US dollars for USA & International and are subject to change without prior notice.
- Orders are shipped surface mail. For courier rates, visit our web-site: **www.companyscoming.com** or contact us: **Tel: (780) 450-6223 Fax: (780) 450-1857**.
- Sorry, no C.O.D's.

Gift Giving

- Let us help you with your gift giving!
- We will send cookbooks directly to the recipients of your choice if you give us their names and addresses.
- Please specify the titles you wish to send to each person.
- If you would like to include your personal note or card, we will be pleased to enclose it with your gift order.
- Company's Coming Cookbooks make excellent gifts: Birthdays, bridal showers, Mother's Day, Father's Day, graduation or any occasion...collect them all!

☐ MasterCard ☐ VISA

Expiry date _____

Account # _____

Name of cardholder _____

Cardholder's signature _____

Shipping Address
Send the cookbooks listed above to:

Name: _____

Street: _____

City: _____ Prov./State: _____

Country: _____ Postal Code/Zip: _____

Tel: ( ) _____

E-mail address: _____

YES! Please send a catalogue: ☐ English ☐ French

Canada's most **popular** cookbooks!